Housetraining That Works

For Dogs of All Ages, Breeds and Backgrounds

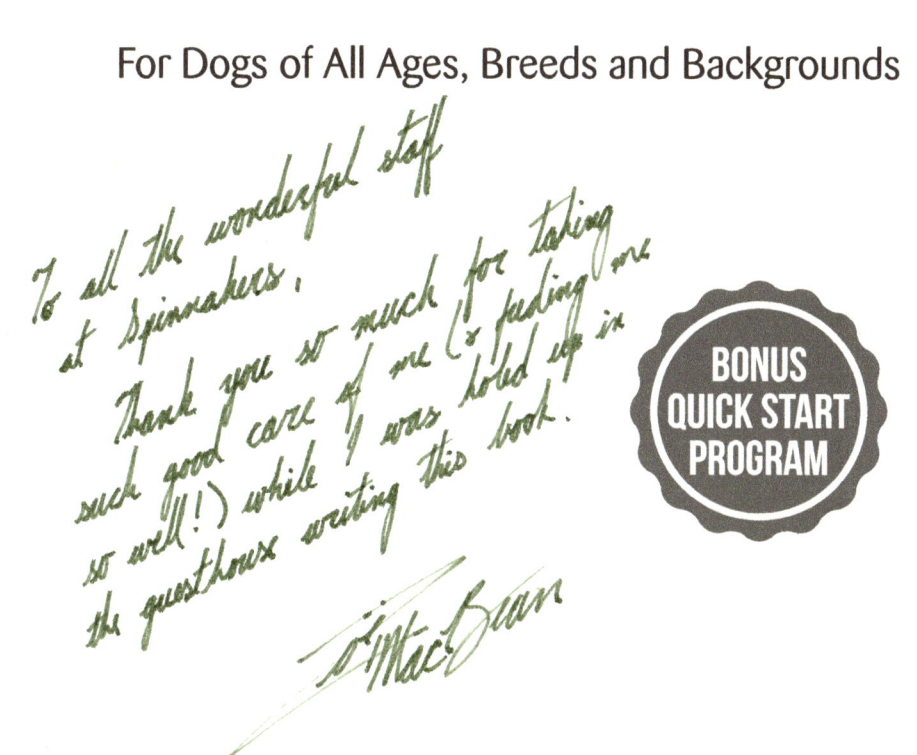

To all the wonderful staff at Spinnakers.

Thank you so much for taking such good care of me (& feeding me so well!) while I was holed up in the guesthouse writing this book.

Zoë MacBean

BONUS QUICK START PROGRAM

Zoë MacBean

First published by Ultimate World Publishing 2024
Copyright © 2024 Zoe Macbean

ISBN

Paperback: 978-1-923255-07-4
Ebook: 978-1-923255-08-1

Zoe Macbean has asserted her rights under the Copyright, Designs and Patents Act 1988 to be identified as the author of this work. The information in this book is based on the author's experiences and opinions. The publisher specifically disclaims responsibility for any adverse consequences which may result from use of the information contained herein. Permission to use information has been sought by the author. Any breaches will be rectified in further editions of the book.

All rights reserved. No part of this publication may be reproduced, stored in or introduced into a retrieval system, or transmitted in any form, or by any means (electronic, mechanical, photocopying, recording or otherwise) without the prior written permission of the author. Any person who does any unauthorized act in relation to this publication may be liable to criminal prosecution and civil claims for damages. Enquiries should be made through the publisher.

Cover design: Ultimate World Publishing
Layout and typesetting: Ultimate World Publishing
Editor: Marnae Kelly
Cover Image Copyright: Odua Images-Shutterstock.com

Ultimate World Publishing
Diamond Creek,
Victoria Australia 3089
www.writeabook.com.au

Praise for Housetraining That Works

"Simply indispensable! This concise, entertaining and simple program ensures a positive start for puppies and adult dogs alike. This book will be sent in advance to any prospective home for my purpose bred Irish Setters. Whether destined for field, show or pet - it's the perfect start for any pup. Housetraining That Works will be in gift baskets for any friends or family welcoming a new companion into their home."

**Susan Russell, preservation breeder, trainer,
CKC life member, Animal Health Technologist**

"This book left me enlightened, inspired and, above all, hopeful. As a dog rescue worker, it fills my heart with joy that this book is rescue dog-inclusive. This challenging training hurdle is covered using relatable experiences, practical strategies and humour, making this book accessible and enjoyable for everyone. A true one-of-a-kind training book, hopefully the first of many to come…"

**Kimberlee Voorspools, Rescue Co-ordinator,
Co-founder of Furever Endeavour Rescue Network**

"As a long term dog breeder and pet manners trainer, I have always searched for a common sense, easy-to-read book on how to start out with a new puppy, in a manner that will avoid issues later in life. Finally I have found it, a simple, well laid out, easy-to-read guide, full of common sense and practical ideas!"

**Ann McPhee, long time breeder and dog fancier,
CKC life member, Trekhond Kennel, Perm. Reg'd**

"Practical, relatable, and eminently readable. So much more than just a 'how to' of housetraining, this book is a gem. New dog families will learn valuable life skills and lay the training foundations for their pup's future adventures, all the while navigating the sometimes tricky business of housetraining. This book will be in all my future puppy packs and on my list of suggested reading for new puppy or rescue homes."

**Rachel Koopman-Gough, Certified Canine Strength and
Conditioning Coach, Canine Bodyworker,
Arohanui Goldens**

For Bowie:
The bestest, bravest, biggest little dog ever.
Squeaka-squeaka, sweet girl.
We miss you.

Contents

Introduction	1
How to Use This Book	3
Chapter 1: Reasons for Accidents	5
Chapter 2: Understanding Your Dog	25
Chapter 3: The Seven-Step System	37
Chapter 4: Potty Profile	43
Chapter 5: Setting Up Your Potty Area	61
Chapter 6: Setting Up Confinement Areas	75
Chapter 7: Teaching Potty Cues	89
Chapter 8: Your Dog's Personal Potty Plan	97
Chapter 9: How to Do a Potty Run	109
Chapter 10: Building Control	125
Chapter 11: Learning a Signal	139
Chapter 12: Handling Accidents	145
Parting Thoughts	153
Quick Start Housetraining Guide	163
Resources	169
Acknowledgments	175
About the Author	179
Speaker Bio	181
Want More?	183

Introduction

Chances are good that if you're reading this, you're spending way too much time cleaning up dog messes, and you're at the end of your leash. Pun intended. So, here's the deal—housetraining problems are totally fixable.

You might also be an extremely clever and forward-thinking person who decided to read up in advance of getting your dog. In a perfect world, you might even have an amazing breeder, shelter or rescue who sent you this book the minute they accepted your deposit to help you give your new family member the best possible start.

The information in this book will work on any dog of any age, breed or background. These methods have been successfully used on dogs from six weeks of age to seventeen years. If your dog has three or more legs, most of its senses (yes, it will work on blind or deaf dogs, too) and a functioning digestive system, you are on your way to a housetrained dog. Take a deep breath. All will be well.

Housetraining That Works

Housetraining is simple, but not always easy—especially at the start. There will be late-night, pre-dawn and I-just-sat-down potty runs. There will be mistakes at the worst possible times and in the worst possible places. There may be times when you wonder why you ever got a puppy or brought home a rescue. All I can tell you is that this phase doesn't last long, and, if you do it right the first time, you'll save yourself a lot of frustration, time and money.

Dog trainers have a lot of stupid jokes about housetraining. We say super helpful things like "It's easy—just don't let them potty in the house." Amazing you let us live, really.

All jokes aside, housetraining rests on just a few key practices. If you feed your dog a food that agrees with them, give them adequate opportunities to go in the right place, reinforce consistently, supervise effectively and confine them safely when your eyes have to be elsewhere, you will succeed.

How to Use This Book

If you haven't brought your puppy home yet, or if housetraining is going well so far, please take the time to read the entire book and complete the checklists. Everything will just make more sense that way.

If you are in crisis and need help right away, please go directly to the Quick Start section at the back of the book and just do what it tells you. When you've had three to five accident-free days, you can go back to the start and read what you've missed. In the meantime, the program will work just fine whether you understand it completely or not.

Housetraining is often seen as something you have to get through before the "real training" begins. It's actually the very beginning of your training relationship. Housetraining is usually where a dog first understands that the human at the other end of the leash is capable of rudimentary communication. That what we do has meaning. That they can get what they want by doing what we want. That we can be trained, too.

Housetraining That Works

If you know what to look for, you may get to observe that first shining moment that your dog understands you are trying to teach them something.

Even if you adopt an adult dog that is already housetrained, you will have to adapt that training to a new environment and your own needs. The process might take less time than for a new puppy, but the steps are the same and so are the training opportunities.

Throughout this book, you will find insights and information meant to deepen your understanding of your dog, and, starting in Chapter 5, you will also find "Sneaky Trainer" sections. Why "sneaky"? Two reasons. First, because all of the behaviours you'll be teaching are rather cunning "proto-behaviours" that can be grown into all manner of useful skills later when you're less exhausted and preoccupied. Stuff that you might not have ever thought to teach. (That's when trainers say things like "Remember when Max was little and we taught him to _____? Now that he's older, let's use that to teach him _____." We play a long game. No apologies.) Second, because it's usually at least two weeks before the dog realizes that not only are we teaching them things, but we have cleverly managed to make it seem like a good idea to go along with our silly games.

If you teach even half of the Bonus Behaviours, you will be light years ahead in your training skills by the time your dog is housetrained, and they will have an educational foundation that will make all future training much easier.

CHAPTER 1

Reasons for Accidents

There are ten reasons that dogs have accidents in the house. Generally, they fall into two categories—physical/medical ones and behavioural ones. Here's the list:

1. Age
2. Medical conditions
3. Nutrition and supplements
4. Background
5. Not clear about where to go (or not to go)
6. Inside too long
7. Don't know how to tell you they need out
8. Fear and anxiety
9. Submissive urination
10. Marking and leg lifting

It's not unusual for dogs to have multiple reasons (especially if they come from a less-than-ideal background), but I promise your dog does not have all ten.

They might have a medical condition. They could be very young or very old. They might never have been inside a house. They might be really anxious. Or they might just not understand that the minute they step out of their sleeping area they're not actually "outside"—at least not by human standards.

It's really important to get a clear picture of your dog's unique challenges before you start your housetraining program so you can focus your efforts. In Chapter 4, you'll find a checklist to help you figure out your pup's "potty profile," but, first, let's explore all ten reasons in depth.

Reason #1: Age

Age really isn't a training issue. It's more of a management issue—allowances and accommodations have to be made until the situation changes. There are a number of age brackets, and each has its own challenges.

Under Seven Weeks

I really don't recommend bringing home a puppy under seven weeks of age—pups need to be with their mamas and litter mates for at least seven weeks. Less than that and you risk all kinds of behavioural repercussions. Sadly, orphaned or abandoned puppies do happen, and sometimes unscrupulous producers will lie about a puppy's age to make a sale.

If you've managed to acquire a puppy under seven weeks old, be aware that they may need some extra help. When puppies are very young, their mothers wash them to stimulate the elimination process and they'll urinate or defecate in response to that washing. If your pup just doesn't seem to be pooping much (usually by five weeks they can manage peeing on their own), you may need to

Reasons for Accidents

take a warm, damp washcloth and gently simulate the mother's tongue licking the urogenital area and anus. That will usually cause them to eliminate. Think that's icky? Count your blessings—mother dogs usually ingest the waste products. You get to skip that part!

Important: *If you have an underage pup in your care, please schedule a vet visit ASAP. Your puppy will very likely need extra nutritional support and medical treatment.*

Seven to Eight Weeks

Seven-to-eight-week-old puppies just don't have much bladder and bowel control at all. There is only a tiny amount of time between when they sense a need to empty their bladder and when it actually happens. Same goes for pooping.

Eight to Twelve Weeks

When they get to the eight-to-twelve-week bracket, you'll get a few more seconds to work with—as in, you might actually have a chance to put your boots on before you go running outside—but it's very individual. Some dogs mature quickly. Others take longer.

I don't care how many of your friends, relatives or neighbours said that their puppy could hold it forever at that age and never had an accident in the house. Housetraining prodigies do happen occasionally, but they're about as common as unicorns and babies who sleep through the night. If your pup can hold it for three seconds, you're doing well.

Housetraining That Works

Teething (twelve weeks to six months)

If you're dealing with a twelve-week-old puppy, you've got about three to thirty seconds notice between when the dog thinks they might have to go and when it's happening *now*. If you brought your puppy home at eight weeks, that's going to seem like a huge improvement!

By now, you may be feeling like you've got the hang of this housetraining stuff, and then, somewhere between twelve and fourteen weeks, serious teething kicks in and your precious pup turns into a shark with paws. Their mouth is on fire, they start chewing everything in sight and they may have accidents—mostly peeing. The most common cause is that they tend to tank up on water in an attempt to soothe the pain.

Bladder infections are also common at this age. It's not unusual for a very distracted-looking pup to just walk over to you and start peeing right in front of you like they've never pottied outside in their life. The only really good news is that the worst of it will be over in a few short weeks. Good luck!

Teen Dogs (five to twenty-four months)

Teen pups sometimes get so distracted by life and living that they just forget themselves. They have good days, and they have bad days. They have days where they're sensible, mature creatures and other days where they seem to have left their brains on another planet. They're just a bit weird—much like human teens. Luckily, this phase doesn't last as long in dogs as it does in humans.

Reasons for Accidents

Adult Dogs

Adult dogs are generally easy to housetrain. Age isn't really the factor here as much as their background is. If you adopt an adult dog from a shelter or a rescue organization, you don't know if that dog has ever been inside a house. There may be a history of punishment that will make it scary for your dog to potty in front of you. Also, people often lie when they drop off dogs.* Sometimes they'll say the dog is house trained when they know it isn't. Sometimes what they really mean is that they had a dog door and the dog used it most of the time. If you don't have a dog door, you may be in trouble. Adult dogs that never went through the process of developing bladder and bowel control have to be treated like very young puppies.

Senior Dogs

Depending on the breed, a dog can be classified as a senior as early as six years. I really don't consider a dog to be senior until they're double digits, but some breeds tend to age prematurely, and the giant breeds have shorter lifespans. Senior dogs often need to go out more often and may need help with mobility challenges like stairs. Pain management is important too. If your senior dog is suddenly having accidents in the house, it's time to go to the vet. Any underlying medical conditions will need to be addressed before going forward.

---

* Every shelter worker knows that "we're moving" is code for "the dog chews, digs, barks, bites or poops in the house."

Reason #2: Medical Conditions

Important: **I am NOT a veterinarian. The following section is not to be construed as medical advice. These are just some things I've observed over the years that may help you know when it's time to ask your veterinarian for help and possibly guide your inquiries.**

Your dog needs to be in good health for housetraining to work. The most common ailments that affect housetraining are diarrhea (usually from too many treats or inappropriate food) and, especially in puppies, worms.

If your dog is only ever peeing in the house, then we have to check for bladder infections or other urinary tract issues. Retriever and Rottweiler girls seem particularly prone to bladder infections when they are teething.

Next up are a couple of nasty single-celled organisms—coccidia and giardia. There are others, but these are the ones that seem to crop up most frequently. If you live near a large population of Canada geese or other waterfowl, or your dog came from less than hygienic conditions, you may want to check for these.

There's a couple of physical symptoms and behavioural "tells" that will prompt me to send a dog to the veterinarian to check for these. Although diarrhea is usually the first symptom listed, the one I see most often is frequent, fully formed but disproportionately large stools—even when feeding a high-quality food. Serious cases can be accompanied by seizures.

The other thing I've noticed consistently is very low learning retention. Dogs that have either one or both of these nasty bugs are quite often

Reasons for Accidents

a little bit on the hyperactive side and have trouble concentrating. Both conditions can be difficult to detect depending on which test is being used. You may have to test two or three times before getting a diagnosis.

Pain can also cause housetraining issues, especially in senior dogs, because it is both distracting and discouraging. If their potty area requires using stairs or is too far away, sometimes it's just easier to pee by the door and go back to bed. If you're seeing an onset of training issues in your senior dog, pain may be playing a large part.

This is by no means an exhaustive list, and chances are your dog is fine, but if you are having issues with housetraining and you're seeing things like excessively large stools, more poops per day than seems reasonable, runny stools, particularly foul smelling stools, urine that looks really dark or urine that has a very bad odour, it's time to call your veterinarian.

Reason #3: Food and Supplements

This is a tricky one. I can't tell you what to feed your dog—that's a term of the trainer's insurance that I carry. Also, I'm not a canine nutritionist (and your veterinarian probably isn't, either). What I can give you are some general rules and some information about how I make feeding decisions for my own dogs.

If your dog has a reasonable number of stools per day, the size of the stools is proportionate to the size of your dog and the stools are well-formed, then leave it alone for now. The start of housetraining is not the time to make major changes to their food without a darn good reason.

Housetraining That Works

If your puppy came from your breeder in good condition and is being fed a food that the breeder recommended but someone (your trainer/neighbour/best friend/pet store clerk/relative/supermarket cashier/some random guy at the coffee shop) suggested a change, think twice. Unless your veterinarian is recommending a change for specific medical reasons, leave it alone for a little bit. I'm going to recommend that you do nothing drastic in the way of changing their diet for at least the first couple of weeks while we are establishing potty cues, toilet areas and routines. The last thing you need is a dog with an upset tummy.

If your dog came from a shelter or rescue, ask what they were being fed and assess for yourself whether a change is in order. Shelter dogs are often fed donated food of varying quality, and it can take a while to get their digestive systems settled down.

Some people want to feed just kibble but give their dogs multiple supplements. Others want to feed just one thing that comes out of a bag from the vet's. Some people cook for their dogs. Some feed raw exclusively. My own dogs are fed a wide variety of foods. Mostly raw. A little freeze-dried or baked kibble when we're travelling. No extruded kibble. A few key supplements. All those options are okay. It's *your* dog and *you* get to choose. Don't let anyone pressure you.*

Be careful about dog food that is very high in protein. I figured this one out years ago when a client's dog ate half a jar of amino acids. Poor little tyke proceeded to ruin a carpet with copious amounts

---

* One of the best resources for learning how to feed and how to understand nutrition labels is a marvellous publication called *Whole Dog Journal*. They take a balanced approach and have rigorous standards for food quality. Their annual review of commercial dog foods is a must-read. A subscription, digital or hard copy, will give you all the tools you need to read labels knowledgeably and make well-informed choices about feeding your dog.

of the stinkiest pee ever. If your dog is urinating frequently and it smells really bad, you might be dealing with too much protein in their food. In addition to making housetraining extra challenging, that's awful hard on their kidneys.

If you're going to feed your dog commercial kibble, choose one with top-quality ingredients. Low-quality food with lots of fillers makes for high stool volume, more frequent pooping and a generally irritated gut, which is seriously unhelpful for housetraining.

What you feed is important, but so is how much you feed. The amount the bag recommends is usually far more than what your dog needs to eat. I've met only a handful of dogs who can actually eat the recommended amount without becoming profoundly obese.

When you feed a dog more than it can use, there are really only a few things their body can do with the excess calories. It can convert them to excess energy, store them as body fat or excrete them. Usually, you'll get a little of all three but young dogs are a little more prone to just pooping more. A lot more.

Reason #4: Background (Birth Environment, Breed and Breeders)

Dogs come into our lives in so many ways. If you're reading this, you probably already have a dog. You might have spent months researching breeds and breeders, adopted from a shelter or found your dog abandoned by the side of the road. Or anything in between. Please don't be distressed if your dog came from a less-than-ideal situation. It's all fixable. Your dog will just need a little more time and patience.

Housetraining That Works

Where your dog came from, their birth environment and living conditions, can have a profound effect on housetraining. Let's take a closer look at some common "origin stories."

Breed:

Your dog's breed has very little to do with housetraining—no matter what anyone says. Yes, it's true that some of the small, fast maturing breeds tend to catch on quickly and some of the large or giant breeds can take longer to develop the necessary control. It's also worth knowing that dogs that tend to look and act like puppies for their whole life (think floppy ears, soft temperaments, baby faces) can also be slow to mature. That doesn't mean they don't get housetrained. They just might take a little longer and need closer supervision.

Breeders:

As far as housetraining is concerned, there's very little variation between breeds but tremendous variation between *breeders*. If the breeder's house smells bad, please don't buy a puppy from them. That's a pretty good indicator that the parent dogs weren't housetrained. The puppies will have learned from them and that can be hard to get past.

If you visit a breeder and they say things like "Oh, well, you know, Pugs can't really be housetrained" or "Frenchies are just like that," please walk away. Don't buy a dog from them. That has nothing to do with the breed and has everything to do with the skills and priorities of the humans. Sometimes that's a really good indication that who you're dealing with doesn't deserve to be called a breeder. They're a *producer*. They're either churning out puppies as fast as they can to take advantage of fad markets, or they really just don't know any better.

Reasons for Accidents

There are excellent breeders out there. Look for a general impression of cleanliness in the puppy area—keeping in mind that "poop happens" and all hell can break loose in the five minutes it took the breeder to answer the door!

Rescue Organizations:

This is a tricky category because rescue organizations come in a lot of "flavours." There are the breed-specific ones that are often affiliated with a kennel club breed association. Some are more grass roots and have a small group of dedicated volunteers doing amazing work with a handful of dogs at a time. There are the combination shelter-transitioning-to-foster-care ones and the amazing full-disclosure rescues that will tell you everything they know about their dogs—the good and the bad. There are organizations that carefully screen homes and work closely with trainers to make sure they don't place a dog with behaviour challenges until it's truly ready and they find a home that is the perfect fit. Sometimes a rescue is a registered non-profit with a board of directors and an operating budget. Other times, it's a couple of dedicated people changing the world one dog at a time. Or anything in between.

These are worthy groups, and you'll know you're dealing with top-notch folks if the dog you're looking at has been fostered in an actual home for at least ten days and if their application form has somewhat challenging questions about your suitability as an adopter and clear expectations for how they expect a dog to be treated while in your care.

Sadly, there are also "retail rescues" that will hide much-needed background information, sugar-coat serious aggression issues and adopt out to anyone willing to pay their fee.

Housetraining That Works

If you've been lucky enough to adopt from a quality rescue, your dog will be well on their way to being housetrained already. Get as much background information as you can and ask for any details about the dog's current potty habits and schedule. Consider making a donation in addition to the adoption fee.

If your dog was flown in from overseas and you met them at the airport, proceed as if you've just brought home a brand-new puppy from a questionable background.

Shelters:

There are shelters that are privately owned, where every dog goes out for daily walks and has their own room with furniture and a television. Those are the exception. Most shelters are understaffed and profoundly underfunded. The dog runs are usually some variation of concrete and chain link, often with no outdoor access. They are run by amazing people who do a lot of good work under seriously challenging conditions but one good sniff of the kennel area will tell you whether they have the resources to make housetraining a priority. If your dog had to use its living area as a bathroom, they will need some patience and understanding while adapting to their new environment.

Pet Stores:

Thankfully, it's very rare now to see dogs sold in pet stores. If you temporarily took leave of your senses and bought the "doggie in the window," be extra aware that being confined to a cage, your dog had no option but to pee and poop in their own living space. And play in it. And get it all over themselves. They likely got pretty used to smelling awful and having yucky stuff on them. Also, it's uncomfortable to hold it all in and it's a relief to let go. Depending

Reasons for Accidents

on how long they were in that environment and where they came from originally, your dog will likely need a lot more time and patience until they learn a "new normal."

Puppy Mills:

Puppy mills mostly operate in two versions. There are the ones where someone has one stud dog and a few females and they're producing a few litters a year because they like the extra cash. They like dogs but don't bother with health testing the parents, and anyone who shows up with money can take one or more home. Hygiene is usually a bit questionable, and pups are often sent home too young. That's bad enough.

Large-scale puppy mills are usually just about money. Sometimes mental health issues play a part. Other times, organized crime gets involved. Most often, it's just a business, and the dogs are seen as a product and nothing more. Whatever the motivation, just imagine large numbers of dogs (often a hundred or more) kept in extremely confined spaces and living in extreme filth. I've been involved in closing down a couple of those operations. The conditions and treatment of the dogs defy description.

Generally speaking, dogs raised in these hellish places are going to be a lot harder to housetrain. They have to get used to feeling clean. They have to get used to the idea that someone is going to take them out, so there's a good reason to hold it. Be patient, consistent and, above all, kind. They've been through enough.

Reason #5: Not Clear About Where to Go (or Not to Go)

The most common reason that dogs have accidents in the house is that they are seriously unclear about where they're actually supposed to go. There are some cultural issues at play here. From a human point of view, the house is inside and the yard is outside. From the dog's point of view, their crate or bed is inside. Anything beyond that is outside and therefore fair game.

Sometimes they'll expand that definition a little bit to include the room with their bed or crate. They'll perhaps keep the kitchen clean, but anything beyond it is outside. If they spend time with their family downstairs, and they're not really allowed upstairs, then upstairs is also outside from the dog's point of view. If somebody leaves the baby gate open, the dog may seize the opportunity for a luxury indoor toilet experience.

Dogs get a lot of mixed messages about housetraining. One of the first is that, in the happy confusion of puppy arrival, the potty area you want your dog to use is rarely the first place the dog goes.

Then there's the confusion over the humans being allowed to go to the bathroom in the house—often in multiple locations. It's very common for dogs to have accidents in their owner's bathrooms—often as close to the toilet as possible. It's also worth noting that it's usually the more intelligent dogs who do this. In the absence of clear information, they solve their problem to the best of their understanding and ability.

Next is indoor housetraining. There can be a lot of really good reasons why you might want to train a dog to use pee pads, paper or even a litter box, especially when they're very young or very small. An indoor area is a smart move anytime you're dealing with issues

Reasons for Accidents

like extreme weather, predators, owner mobility challenges or long elevator rides, to name just a few.

The problems usually start when transitioning the dog from pee pads to outdoors because it makes no sense to the dog. You've basically told them that it's okay to potty in the house as long as it's in this one (or two or three) tiny little square. They've never had to develop bladder or bowel control because they always had unlimited access. Now you want them to hold it long enough to commute to the new place, brave the elements, ignore the distractions of the outdoors and maybe even have to go on leash, with you looking.

Your house may also be giving a mixed message. Unless it's brand new, houses have histories. Often, smelly pet-related histories. We once had a dog who was a little prone to pee accidents stemming from serious puppyhood bladder infections. She was having the occasional accident in the far corner of the house that overlooked the backyard. My first thought was that she'd been inside too long, got caught short and problem-solved to the best of her ability by going as close to the right spot as she could get.

What that didn't explain was how many visiting dogs would walk over to that corner and pee—to their owner's absolute shock and horror. That's probably the most times I've ever heard "He's never done that before!"

Then one day, my daughter's new friend walked into the house and said, "Oh! I remember this place. I used to live here. My dog had puppies right over there." Mystery solved.

If your otherwise perfectly housetrained dog has one spot they just can't resist, there might be a perfectly reasonable explanation.

Special note:

Breeders who keep a puppy from their latest litter are often embarrassed that all the pups they sent home are housetraining rock stars while the one they kept is frustratingly slow to catch on. It's perfectly understandable—your puppy is living in its original toilet environment. While all the others have gone home to novel environments that are set up for success (thanks to all your hard work), yours is still living in or near an area that is pretty much constantly signalling, "Potty here!" You didn't do anything wrong—stop beating yourself up. You'll get there. It's just going to take a little more time.

Reason #6: Inside Too Long

This one's pretty straightforward. The only real challenge is that humans quite often will have a different idea about what is "too long" versus what their dog would tell them. This is not actually up to you because it is dictated by your dog's individual ability to hold it, and that's influenced by a lot of factors such as age, medical issues and nutrition.

There are dogs with seemingly multi-dimensional bladders, but there are others that need to go out every two to four hours. Some dogs get really excited anticipating their owners coming home. That excitement generates more movement, and the movement tends to make them need to pee. When the owner is ten minutes late, there may be a "welcome home" puddle by the door.

Hormone cycles and pregnancy also affect how long they can wait— just like humans. So, if you have intact female dogs, there will be times when they need to go out more frequently.

Reasons for Accidents

Reason #7: Don't Know How to Tell You They Need Out

Your dog may not know how to tell you, or that they even *should* tell you, that they need to go out. They may not even know that telling you is an option.

Another possibility is they think they did tell you, but it was so subtle you didn't notice.

Lastly, it could be they're afraid to tell you—which is a nice segue to the next reason.

Reason #8: Fear and Anxiety

The most common cause of fear-related accidents is a history of being scolded. This one is particularly problematic because your dog will not connect the punishment with the *act* of going to the bathroom in the house. From their point of view, you plus the *presence* of poop or pee is an accurate predictor for getting in trouble. That makes it many times harder for the dog to relax enough to potty in front of you, which in turn increases the chances of accidents.

It gets worse: your dog can become so fearful of you coming home and yelling at them that they start being fearful of what they're hearing or seeing or smelling outside. Care to guess what dogs do when they're anxious? They potty in the house. (Okay, they also bark, chew and dig, but that's a topic for another book.)

We humans tend to "whistle in the dark" or turn on all the lights if we get spooked watching a scary movie so that our environment instantly looks and sounds more familiar. Dogs are less visual and more olfactory, so when they get scared they like to make their space *smell* less scary. If they're just a little fearful, they usually handle that by peeing in the house. Truly terrifying stuff will literally scare the sh*t out of them.

Another common source of fear, and the most overlooked one, is a dog having too much space to look after. In a misguided effort to be extra caring, some folks give their dogs way too much space at bedtime or when they're left home alone. Instead of a nice, cozy crate or modest pen, they'll leave them loose in a larger room or even the whole house.

Dogs have some interesting cultural values around space and territory. If they're given too much of it too soon, they often become anxious. It's a big responsibility and not usually a welcome one. If they hear, smell or see something outside that makes them feel like they might have to defend that space, they tend to pee or poop just because it makes them feel better. A way of saying, "Hey, you big scary thing out there, I've marked this space because I'm really a badass and not a quivering scaredy-cat!"

While we're on the subject of things that go bump in the night, it is surprisingly common for dogs to be scared of the dark. If your housetraining woes began when the nights got longer, maybe check that your dog is actually going out in the yard to potty and not just house-hugging the porch light and waiting to be let in.

Finally, if you have a dog who's normally very well housetrained but has suddenly started having accidents, especially when you're away, you may have to do some sleuthing. There may be something weird going on. Blasting, fireworks or thunderstorms are really common causes. Where I live, it's often that the bears have come out of hibernation and they're prowling around in the yard. Wildlife cameras and doorbell cameras may reveal anything from large predators to weird neighbours and everything in between!

Reasons # 9: Submissive Urination

This is the one where your dog gets excited and squats to pee when guests arrive. It can also happen when you or a friend reach down to pet them. Although the problem can persist in older dogs, it's most common in puppies. It's part of a range of appeasing behaviours designed to switch off aggression and keep pups safe by signalling their non-threatening status. Typically, they get over it by the time they're a year old if it's ignored and gently managed.

Owners are often horrified or embarrassed by submissive urination, but it's important to recognize that this is a perfectly normal dog behaviour. It's sort of the canine equivalent of blushing. Also, in very much the way blushing is made worse by someone paying attention to it, so is submissive urination.

Reason #10: Marking and Leg Lifting

Although male dogs are more prone to it, both female and male dogs can leg lift to mark territory. If your dog is peeing on upright things in your house, and that's all they're ever doing, that's marking their territory.

Sometimes dogs will also mark territory by peeing on horizontal surfaces like couch cushions or the middle of your bed—something that smells strongly of you or another dog. That behaviour is more common to female dogs, and it's more often an anxiety response, but that isn't always the case.

That One Other Reason

If you're wondering why there's nothing on the list about "doing it out of spite" or "being angry they were left alone," it's because those reasons don't exist. Dogs don't even have the part of the brain needed to execute a plan based on malice, revenge or spite.

This non-reason has been the justification for countless dogs being punished, dumped at shelters or euthanized for the simple crime of not understanding or being afraid. Let's put it to rest once and for all.

CHAPTER 2

Understanding Your Dog

Now that you know why dogs have accidents in the house and which of those reasons applies to your dog in particular, it's time to backtrack a little and learn a bit more about dog culture, biology and behaviour.

You've likely been inundated with helpful information from any number of sources. Perhaps you bought a book or even a few books. Maybe even read them. You might have downloaded tip sheets off the internet, asked your obedience class trainer (or your breeder or a friend or your neighbour or good old Uncle Fred), and you're now thoroughly confused. Some of what they told you may be right, but some of it could be horrifyingly wrong. I'm going to suggest that you choose one source of information for your housetraining and go with that. Like maybe this book.

Housetraining That Works

How Dogs Learn

So, training isn't rocket science, but there are some basics you have to know. Dogs learn by getting it right and getting rewarded or reinforced. They don't learn by punishment. Well, that's not quite true. They do learn something by being punished, but it sure isn't what you wanted them to learn. (More on that later.)

Regardless of what you want to train your dog to do, you will need to show them what you want or create a situation where the behaviour is likely to occur and reward them *promptly* when they do it. Don't assume your dog understands what you want.

When it comes to housetraining, it's even better if you assume they *don't* understand and take full responsibility for making the right behaviour happen whether you're housetraining a puppy, getting an adult shelter dog accustomed to life indoors, or re-training an elderly dog. As the old saying goes, "Practice makes permanent," so it's best to be vigilant about preventing them from doing anything you don't want.

You may have been told that dogs are easy to housetrain because they're den animals. That they have a natural tendency to keep their dens clean, so all you have to do is take them outside regularly. That's fine when it works. Where the problems start is that we are primates and tend to prefer open spaces and vantage points over the cozy, dark hiding spots favoured by dogs. It's really easy for us to lose track of what a dog thinks of as a safe, secure den.

For a dog, a den space is just big enough for them to go in, curl up and lie down. For the seriously pack-oriented pup, that might also include enough room for the rest of their littermates to curl up and lie down. Anything beyond that is "outside." To help you understand, let's take a look at where housetraining begins—with your dog's mother.

Understanding Your Dog

Where It All Begins

Housetraining usually starts with the mother dog. When puppies are small, the mother dog is responsible for keeping the den clean because, for the first couple weeks, puppies aren't physically able to leave the den to go to the bathroom. After nursing, the mother licks the urogenital area of each pup, and this stimulates the puppies to eliminate. They'll pee and poop, and mom cleans it up by ingesting the waste.

At the earliest possible chance (and can you blame her?) when the puppies first start to toddle, the mother dog will walk away from the den area a little bit and encourage the puppies to follow her. Quite often she will leave the den area when the pups are hungry, so the puppies have to follow her to eat. When they've done nursing, she'll lick them clean, and that stimulates them to go to the bathroom.

Really quickly, puppies figure out that sleeping happens in one area, eating happens there or just beyond it, and then we go somewhere else to go to the bathroom. When the pups are able to walk, they begin standing to nurse. At this point, sleeping, eating and pottying become even more separated both in time and location.

As there are usually distinct differences in surface for the den/sleeping area vs. the eating/play/potty areas, this is also when the first tactile preferences come in. That is, the puppy differentiates the areas not only by smell and location but by how the space feels under their paws. "Outside" is defined by many pups as "the place that feels different than where I sleep."

If your pup came from a well-informed breeder, they may have used blankets, towels or hospital pads for the sleeping area and something else for the potty area—like wood shavings, linoleum or grass. Whatever surface the puppies stepped on immediately beyond their sleeping area was their first toileting area, and they will have imprinted on that as a kind of tactile memory.

So, when you're housetraining a puppy, it's actually quite helpful to know what they first peed and pooped on—because that's going to be what attracts them. For instance, if they've never peed on grass, but the whelping area had tile or linoleum, you're going to find it a challenge keeping that puppy clean in your kitchen because that's the tactile surface that says, "Hey, this is a good place to go."

The same is true of puppies raised on a single type of surface. With no defined difference between the den and the rest of their world, puppies will just wander off a short distance and squat. If your pup came from a shelter or a less-than-ideal producer, be aware that they will need a little extra time and help to understand where to go and where not to go.

The best breeders support their mama dogs' efforts to housetrain their pups, and it makes a huge difference. If you're lucky enough to get a pup from such an enlightened soul, you have a head start on the road to housetraining success.

You also need to understand that if you've just rescued a dog or a puppy from a really questionable situation, they may be used to living in their own filth and may never have learned to hold it in. You'll have to watch them very carefully, and they'll need a lot of help just to learn that it's nice to be clean.

The Gastrocolic Reflex

The other thing you need to know about is a little something called the gastrocolic reflex. This is a digestive process that helps keep waste

Understanding Your Dog

products moving along. It also means that if your puppy puts anything at all in their mouth—whether that's food, water, a bug, your socks or a toy—for any significant amount of time, something will come out the other end.

Whether your dog is triggered to pee, poop or both will vary. Technically, the gastrocolic reflex only covers pooping, but almost everything that can make a dog poop can also make them pee, so we'll just roll with that.

If you want to understand your dog and why they are having accidents in the house, it really helps to understand what makes them poop and pee in the first place. Almost everyone knows that waking up, eating and drinking can stimulate a dog to need the bathroom, but if you want your dog housetrained as fast as possible, you need to know *everything* that can trigger them to potty. The list is reasonably short, but there may be a few surprises:

1. Waking up
2. Eating a meal
3. Drinking
4. Getting ready to sleep
5. Chewing
6. Treats
7. Playing (especially games that involve a mouth on an object)
8. Walking or exercise
9. Stress
10. People or dogs arriving or leaving
11. Meeting another dog or animal
12. Coming home

Housetraining That Works

The first four are easy to understand because they're pretty much the same for humans. The next three are less obvious. Eight through twelve are rarely mentioned. Here's a quick run-through:

Waking Up

You probably know that your dog needs to go to the bathroom when they wake up because, generally speaking, so do we. Puppies in particular may need to pee or poop more than once—their bodies have done a lot of growth and repair work while they slept, and the byproducts of that work need to exit.

Pro Tip: If you have a bit of a "commute" to the potty area, it's wise to take two minutes to empty your own bladder before heading outside. Nothing like a long elevator ride and locking yourself out when there's nothing open and you're in pyjamas to start your day off badly. Don't ask me how I know.

Eating

When dealing with young puppies, just assume that within a few seconds or minutes after eating, they are going to need to go out to empty themselves. Make sure you allow yourself enough time for the post-feeding potty run before you have to leave or get children off to school or bed.

Adult dogs usually have a little more control. Some go outside first thing for a pee, come back in for breakfast, wait a civilized amount of time and then need to go back out promptly for a poop and another pee. Some are reluctant to go out until they've had breakfast. Others dash outside for a couple of poops first thing and only then will they pee. Take note of your adult dog's "potty style" because the basic pattern usually lasts for their lifetime.

Understanding Your Dog

You do get a little more notice and time to put your shoes on as they get older.

Drinking

This one's pretty straightforward. Your dog might be able to take a few sips and not need to dash outside, but watch out for "tanking up." Young dogs will often over-drink when teething in an attempt to relieve tooth and gum pain.

Adult dogs are most likely to over-drink when they are too hot—because their tongues act as radiators, and they're attempting to cool themselves by cooling their tongues. Filling the bowl with ice cubes and providing a cooling mat will go a long way towards keeping them comfortable.

Important: Please don't let your dog "tank up" on water if they come inside panting from heavy exercise. Offer them half a dozen room-temperature slurps and get them cooled off first before you let them have more.

Getting Ready to Sleep

It's really common for dogs to need the bathroom right before they go to sleep. It's a natural function of them being den animals. Pooping on your den mates is culturally frowned on, so right before they go to bed, they need to go outside. Young puppies in particular can be resistant to going out in the evenings. They're tired, mentally and physically, so they'd really rather not and will tell you they don't need to go. Don't believe them.

Housetraining That Works

Chewing

Dogs' bodies don't seem to understand the difference between chewing and eating. So, if your dog has been chewing, even if they didn't ingest any of the object of dental devotion, treat them as if they've had a meal. When they stop chewing, they need to be whisked outside.

Treats

While some dogs can work you over for a fistful of snacks and not need to go outside to potty, there are others for whom getting even a single treat can trigger the gastrocolic reflex. You'll quickly learn which kind you have!

Important: Treats should be quite small—about the size of your pinky fingernail for an average to large dog. Less for small dogs. If your treats can't be easily broken into something that small, choose a different treat.

Playing

It's really common for people to be playing with their dog in the back yard and then, when someone loses interest or gets tired or the phone rings, everyone goes back inside and two minutes later the dog has an accident. It's a best practice to shut down play a few minutes before you need to go in, settle the pup a little, then take them to their potty area and cue them to go to the bathroom. Same rules apply when your dog is playing with another dog. (More on teaching those cues later on.)

Understanding Your Dog

Walking or Exercise

This is a tricky one because people quite often take their dogs out for exercise to get them to go to the bathroom. Often the dog won't go, so they come home and take the dog inside, and next thing you know there's an accident in the house.

Some dogs are very reluctant to go to the bathroom outside of their home territory, especially when they're young or shy. It's a dog culture thing not to draw attention to yourself if you're a bit vulnerable. When you come back from a walk, always take them to their potty area and cue them so that they can have a chance to go to the bathroom before they go back inside.

Stress

Stress can be caused by any number of things. It could be you frantically running around grabbing your keys and your lunch because you're late for work and dashing out the door.

It could also be scary animals outside your window. We used to live in a very high-predator area, and one of the ongoing stresses was bears literally at our front door. If you're a dog, having a bear looking through your front window or hanging out on your front step is seriously stressful. Same goes for bobcats, cougars, wolves and eagles—anything that looks at them like they're a snack.

Then there's noise stress like fireworks, thunderstorms, roadwork, someone loudly banging on your door when you're away—or you having an argument with your spouse about who was supposed to take the dog out!

Housetraining That Works

There are all kinds of stressors that can really upset dogs. Some of them are visual. Some of them are auditory. There are even scent and tactile stressors. Identify and eliminate as many of them as possible.

Lastly, understand the double-edged sword of stressful things outside your home because those are going to both stimulate your dog to need the bathroom *and* make them reluctant to go outside to pee or poop.

In Chapters 5 and 6, you will learn how to set up safe and comfortable potty areas and confinement areas.

People or Dogs Arriving or Leaving

People raising young or very subordinate dogs usually know to take their dogs out before guests arrive so the dog doesn't get excited and submissively pee. What they often don't realize is that after people arrive, the fuss settles down and everyone is seated, it's very common for the dog to have an accident—and it has nothing to do with submissive urination.

In dog culture, when friendly visitors arrive, you have a big reunion, and everyone goes outside to pee. If your company has traveled a long way, one of the first things they may want to do is use your restroom to "freshen up." Your dog would prefer that everyone went out to the backyard and had a big group toileting event, complete with evaluating each other's efforts, but that's hardly practical. Just let your dog out to pee* shortly after guests arrive.

---

* They probably don't need to poop unless they're really excited or frightened. Fear tends to make dogs need to poop. If your dog finds people alarming, they may need to have an extra bowel movement shortly after company arrives.

Understanding Your Dog

When guests leave, dogs will quite often want to go mark their territory once more to re-designate it as a family space rather than a group rendezvous space. Make sure you let them out again.

All the same rules apply if your visitors are dogs. If your dog has friends over to play or your guests brought a dog, be doubly vigilant. Watch carefully for signs that your dog would really rather be elsewhere—because we don't need to add anxiety to your housetraining challenges. Be especially alert for young male dogs egging each other on in a literal "pissing contest."

The rules are a little different for any visitors that your dog deems unfriendly, whether dog, human or otherwise. In that case, they would usually prefer a solo pee run and a perimeter check to make sure their space is still safe.

If you have multiple dogs, and some are staying home while others are being exercised, make sure everyone gets out for a quick pee just before you leave and right after you get home.

As they get older and more successful in their housetraining, it may become unnecessary to toilet your dog after every coming and going in much the same way that sometimes there's one family member who cannot be bothered to get off the couch to greet guests or say their goodbyes.

Meeting Another Dog

If you're out on a walk, and your dog meets another dog, yours will likely want to go pee. It's rarely a problem unless they meet just as you arrive home. If you stopped to chat with a friendly neighbour and their sweet old retriever, make sure your dog gets a chance to pee before they go back inside.

Onward!

So far, you've learned why dogs have accidents, how they learn, how their mother and their environment shaped their early housetraining and what triggers them to poop or pee.

Next, you'll be learning a simple seven-step system that is the framework for housetraining any dog.

CHAPTER 3

The Seven-Step System

Now it's time for an overview of the simple yet "no stone unturned" system for successfully housetraining any healthy dog, regardless of age, breed or background. Each step will get an in-depth look in the chapters to follow.

Ready? Here are the "bones" of the program:

1. Diagnose the whys
2. Eliminate any medical or food issues
3. Choose and set up potty and confinement areas
4. Train your dog to potty on cue and on leash
5. Create your dog's personal potty plan
6. Build control
7. Learn a signal

Now, let's take a brief look at each of those steps:

Step One: Diagnose the Whys

Knowing the reasons your dog is having accidents is important. Partly so we can understand our dogs and be more patient, or to uncover and address any potential health issues, but mostly so we can achieve **the best results in the shortest amount of time with the least effort.**

There's no point in struggling with your dog's behaviour as a housetraining issue when what they really have is a medical problem. Likewise, there's no point in getting upset that your dog isn't housetrained yet if they're only twelve weeks old. You can save yourself a lot of time and frustration if you figure out exactly what you're dealing with and tailor your approach accordingly. In the next chapter, you'll learn how to pinpoint your dog's particular challenges.

Step Two: Eliminate Any Medical Problems or Food-Related Issues

You cannot housetrain a dog who has diarrhea or a bladder infection. Serious pain and ongoing illness can also make the process more challenging. These are not training issues. In order to succeed, we need a dog who is in the best possible health.

Whether you feed raw, kibble or home-cooked, it is vital that the food sit well with your dog. Some dogs have cast-iron stomachs while others are more tender-tummied. Whatever you feed, make sure it isn't making the situation worse. Choose the best quality food you can afford, bearing in mind that your dog's body gets the final say! The goal is to keep irritation to a minimum and eliminate any unnecessary stress on their gut while supporting optimum health.

The Seven-Step System

Step Three: Set Up Potty and Confinement Areas

You are going to need a safe, inviting place for your dog to go to the bathroom and at least one safe, somewhat restricted area for your dog to hang out in between potty runs.

Potty Areas

For the potty area, it has to both feel safe and be safe. It needs to be as inviting as possible, and it has to be kind of a no-brainer to get there. A straight line from where your dog exits the house works best. Essentially, we want a nice, clean, comfortable and inviting bathroom area so your dog will want to go there and associate that space with relief and good things.

Confinement Areas

In addition to a safe place to go to the bathroom, your dog will need a couple safe spaces to hang out: one for when you can supervise and one for when you can't.

The size and configuration of those spaces will depend a lot on whether you have a brand-new puppy or a "new to you" dog. Puppy areas are generally smaller and more portable—like crates or pens. Older dogs usually don't go as frequently and may be able to handle a bit more space. Designing ideal versions of both spaces will be covered in detail in Chapters 5 and 6.

Step Four: Train Your Dog to Potty on Cue and on Leash

We teach our dogs how to go to the bathroom on leash so that we can control *where* the behaviour occurs. We teach them to do it on cue so we can see *when* the behaviour happens and reinforce it right away. This will create a distinct contrast between when the behaviour happens in the right spot and when it happens off-leash or in the wrong place—because we don't reinforce those.

It's been said that nothing succeeds like success. That's because success gets rewarded. This step is all about knowing when and how to reinforce your dog and how to avoid accidentally reinforcing the wrong behaviours.

The hows and whys of teaching this essential behaviour will be covered in depth in Chapter 7.

Step Five: Create Your Dog's Personal Potty Plan

Your dog is unique, and designing their potty plan requires an understanding of their individual needs. Once you know what to look for, three to five days of careful observation will give you the information you need to create a feeding and toileting schedule that works for both of you.

It's important to recognize that your dog has no idea that your end goal is having them only potty outside or in a designated place indoors. That means you are the only one who can be held responsible for any accidents. Trainers refer to those mistakes as "handler errors." Eliminating as many of them as possible is absolutely key to housetraining success. Good record-keeping, especially in the first thirty days, can help you see important patterns and avoid common pitfalls.

We'll look at how to best set yourself up for success in Chapter 8.

The Seven-Step System

Step Six: Build Control

The final step of housetraining is to develop your dog's bladder and bowel control so you don't have to take them out every half hour for the rest of their life. For young puppies, this is largely a matter of time—they just need to mature a little. For adult dogs, it's usually more about their history and might take a little longer. Regardless of their age, it's important to understand that every dog is an individual. Yours may be a virtuoso of holding it, or they may need a little less time between excursions.

Chapter 10 will discuss some useful behaviours we can introduce that will help your dog develop the best possible control in the shortest amount of time.

Step Seven: Learn a Signal

Once your dog knows where to go, when to go and how to go on cue, life gets a little easier. You'll be able to predict their needs fairly accurately and start giving them a little freedom when they're empty. At this point, it's really useful if your dog has a way to tell you they need to go out because it is all too easy to lose track of time and then find an accident by the exit door.

Details on how to choose and teach a signal can be found in Chapter 11.

What next?

In the next chapter, we'll be figuring out your dog's "potty profile" to find out how many reasons for accidents you're dealing with.

Housetraining That Works

That information will allow you to save time and tailor your approach.

Remember, your dog doesn't have all ten of those reasons. I've met a few sevens and an occasional eight but never a ten or even a nine. Please don't worry—no matter how many boxes you tick, everything's going to be okay.

Ideally, you'll have time to go through the potty profile and learn how to fix each type of housetraining challenge, but if you are in a housetraining crisis, please turn to the Quick Start section right away. Follow the steps and you'll be fine. You can always come back later and read the rest of the book for a better understanding.

CHAPTER 4

Potty Profile

Now that you know all the reasons dogs have accidents, it's time to diagnose why *your* dog is having accidents in the house. Take a look at the list below and check any boxes that apply to your situation.

Don't be alarmed if your dog seems to have a lot of reasons for accidents. That's normal and usually easier to fix than a dog who just has one very specific situation where they slip up because when they're having frequent accidents for a lot of reasons, it's easy to track your progress as the number of accidents drops. If your dog is only having an accident once in a blue moon, it can be difficult to tell if what you're doing is working. (Until you're home sick one day and catch the local cat mafia taunting your dog through the window!)

Housetraining That Works

Age

☐ My dog is under eight weeks old*

☐ My doing is 8–12 weeks old*

☐ My dog is 12–20 weeks old*

☐ My dog is 5–12 months old

☐ My dog is six (or more) years old

☐ My dog is ten (or more) years old

To housetrain a dog when age is a factor, you will need to complete steps 1–6, and you should probably do all seven. In addition, if your dog is a young puppy, you will need to let them grow up. If your dog is a senior, you may need to adjust your expectations and provide them with more assistance as they age.

Medical

Important: If you tick any box in this section, a trip to the vet is in order before you do anything else.

☐ Diarrhea

☐ Constipation/straining

☐ Excessive stool volume

* If you ticked a box with an asterisk, age is *definitely* a factor. If you ticked a box without an asterisk, age *may* be a factor.

Potty Profile

- ☐ Excessive stool frequency
- ☐ Excessive urination
- ☐ Really stinky urine
- ☐ Blood in the urine
- ☐ Blood in the stool
- ☐ Evidence of worms in the stool
- ☐ Difficulty getting up or walking
- ☐ Visibly limping
- ☐ Excessive panting, even when cool
- ☐ Difficulty navigating stairs
- ☐ Restless during normal sleeping hours
- ☐ Sudden change in behaviour

NB: This is by no means a complete list. If you suspect something isn't right, please take your dog for a comprehensive physical.

Nutrition

Note: This one is really, really important, but be careful because until you've ruled out medical issues, you can't start evaluating their food.

Housetraining That Works

☐ I recently changed my dog's food

☐ I recently added a supplement to my dog's food

☐ My dog is eating an economy dog food

☐ I feed my dog the amount recommended on the bag

☐ My dog's food is high in protein

☐ My dog's food has a lot of fractioned ingredients*

☐ I give my dog an oil supplement

☐ I give my dog a vitamin or mineral supplement

If you checked one or more boxes on this list, nutrition *may* be a factor.

Background

☐ My dog came from a shelter

☐ My dog was raised in a very confined space

☐ My dog was raised on a single type of surface

☐ My dog came from a pet store

☐ My dog came from a puppy mill

* similar ingredients listed in slightly different forms

Potty Profile

☐ My dog was kept in dirty conditions

☐ My dog's parents weren't housetrained

☐ My dog has an unknown background

☐ My dog has never been inside a house

☐ My dog was chained

☐ My dog was originally paper-trained

To housetrain a dog whose background is less than ideal, you will need to complete steps 1–6, and you should probably do all seven. In addition, you may need to be extra patient as your dog adjusts to a new and happier normal. If your dog experienced trauma, neglect or abuse, you may need to make additional concessions or accommodations.

Dog Doesn't Understand Where They Should Go

☐ My dog will poop or pee anywhere in the house when I'm home

☐ My dog will poop or pee anywhere in the house when I'm gone

☐ My dog often doesn't go when I take them out

☐ My dog often goes the minute I take my eyes off them

☐ My dog often goes shortly after I bring them back inside

☐ My dog is being transitioned from an indoor to an outdoor potty spot

Housetraining That Works

☐ My dog often doesn't go outside even if the door is open

☐ My dog hides to go to the bathroom

To retrain this dog, you will need to complete all seven steps, paying particular attention to steps 3, 4 & 5.

Inside Too Long (or no access to their bathroom area for too long)

☐ My dog usually has accidents right by the door

☐ My dog has accidents in the bathroom

☐ My dog only has accidents when alone for more than a couple hours

This dog is functionally housetrained. While all the steps would be helpful, step 4 would allow you to be sure your dog was fully empty before leaving, and step 6 would help you develop a signal so your dog can communicate their needs. If you are unable to take your dog out more frequently, it may also be useful to provide an indoor option when your dog has to be alone for longer than they can hold it.

Doesn't Know How to Tell You They Need Out

☐ Most of my dog's accidents happen when I'm distracted

☐ I can't tell when my dog needs to go out

☐ My dog has accidents by the door

Potty Profile

This is more of an owner-training issue. Completing all seven steps with a particular emphasis on steps 4–7 will help you understand your dog better and teach you to observe more closely.

Fear and Anxiety

Please note: Your dog may have generalized anxiety or a specific anxiety about something not listed below.

☐ My dog doesn't have accidents if I leave them in their crate or one small area

☐ My dog pees or poops right in the middle of the room

☐ My dog poops or pees right in the middle of my bed

☐ My dog only has accidents during fireworks or thunderstorms

☐ My dog only has accidents during hunting season

☐ I live in an area with medium or large predators

☐ I have a lot of raccoons in my area (or crows, ravens, squirrels…)

☐ The local cats torment my dog

☐ My dog goes berserk when the delivery person or mail carrier comes to the door

☐ My house is an open floor plan

☐ My dog was recently given access to a larger area when they're alone

Housetraining That Works

☐ My house tends to echo

☐ My neighbours are noisy/always fighting

☐ We are a loud family

☐ Our dog appears anxious if we argue

☐ Someone in our house really dislikes the dog

☐ We recently acquired a new dog (or other pet)

☐ Our pets don't get along with each other

☐ We recently lost a dog

☐ We recently added a new person to our household

☐ A person recently left our household

To train this dog, complete all seven steps. Teach all of the bonus behaviours, as they will help your dog understand that you are there to help and can be counted on to respond predictably. Pay particular attention to developing supervision and confinement practices. In addition, remove as many sources of stress as possible. Make sure your dog is getting enough sleep. Create visual barriers to limit your dog's access to scary visuals. Earplugs can be very helpful for noise-sensitive dogs. In serious cases, medication may be helpful.

Potty Profile

Submissive Urination

☐ My dog squats and pees when guests arrive

☐ My dog pees when scolded

☐ My dog pees when people bend over to greet or pet them

☐ My dog pees when greeted by someone they haven't seen for a long time

Strictly speaking, this isn't a housetraining issue. It's a maturity and confidence issue. If this is the only section you ticked, the only step that you really need is step 4 because having a way to get your dog empty before and after guests arrive is very helpful.

In addition, you will need to advocate for your dog and ask people to ignore them until they're calmer and not to bend over them for petting. It's worth saying again that punishing or scolding will make submissive peeing much worse. Even looking annoyed or disappointed may hinder progress if your dog is very sensitive to micro-facial expressions.

For years, the prevailing advice has been to completely ignore submissive urination and hope they grow out of it eventually. That works pretty well, but it can take a while. Submissive urination should be taken as a compliment. It's an appeasing behaviour designed to signal their vulnerability and demonstrate that they are no threat to higher-ranking, larger and scarier you. Its function is to switch off any aggressive behaviour.

While it's true that if you scold them or punish them in any way, the behaviour will get much worse (we're talking belly-up, tail-distributed fountains of pee here), no one ever seems to acknowledge that ignoring a very young puppy that is doing appeasing gestures can also be construed as scary. As in, "They still don't look happy, maybe I should do it *more*." Because the way it works in dog culture is that puppies appease, beg, roll over and pee until the adult dog *acknowledges them*.

So, while every good trainer I know tells people to ignore submissive urination, what they actually do is quite different. In practice, every one of them will acknowledge the puppy or dog, express some level of delight—"We peed! Yay!"—while simultaneously softening their body language, casting their eyes off to one side and reaching for the cleaning supplies. All of which effectively signals the pup that we are easy to please, so next time they could maybe pee a little less. Is it faster? Maybe, maybe not. But it's lots easier to do than ignoring them. Experiment a little and let your dog's behaviour give you the answer.

<u>Marking and Leg Lifting</u>

☐ My dog only ever pees in the house, never poops

☐ My dog pees on upright objects in the house

☐ My dog is likely to pee on new objects in a familiar environment

☐ My dog will pee on familiar objects when moved to a new location

☐ My dog has lifted his leg on other dogs

☐ My dog has lifted his leg on people

Potty Profile

☐ My dog has lifted his leg in other people's homes

☐ My dog lifts his leg frequently on walks

☐ My dog lifts his leg after every dog-to-dog interaction

☐ My dog spends more time peeing than interacting with humans or dogs

☐ My dog pees in the middle of my bed

☐ My dog will pee on other dogs' beds

☐ My dog has peed on my couch or chair cushions

To housetrain a dog that marks or leg-lifts in the house, you will have to complete all seven steps. In addition, you will have to get clarity on why your dog feels compelled to mark. Indoor leg-lifting is usually assumed to be dominance-related, but that is rarely the case. Anxiety, stress and lack of supervision during adolescent hormone surges are more likely to have played a part. What might have started as a couple of accidents soon becomes an entrenched, scent-cued habit.

Marking and leg-lifting are often assumed to be exclusively male dog behaviours, but females can do both, too. While it's a rare female that marks on vertical objects indoors, they are quite prone to marking dead centre on beds, chairs and sofas. Again, this is rarely anything to do with dominance and everything to do with feeling anxious, stressed or intimidated.

Sometimes an adolescent female will be in conflict, often subtle, with another female of similar social status. Another common scenario is when an older female will "issue a statement" about the presence

Housetraining That Works

and ill manners of a brand-new pup in the household. It isn't malice directed at the pup, and it isn't spite aimed at you. It just means the girl in question is feeling a bit threatened and will need you to be clear about their status and safety within the household.

For dogs, connection and social status in their family pack are intimately connected to survival instincts. Any indication that they have been demoted or ousted may trigger anxiety about their own safety. It is far too easy to dismiss their behaviour as "jealousy" when they are more likely responding to a deeply coded message that says, "loss of social status = danger."

If there is no dog-to-dog conflict in the household, then the most likely triggers are tension between dog and owner or stress in the household. If dogs could send emails or text messages, you'd likely receive something quite cross and written in all caps, but the only tool they have to communicate is their behaviour. From a dog culture perspective, female marking is a non-violent way of expressing serious displeasure at the way their home and family are operating. Peeing on a bed is seriously aggravating, but I'll take that over aggression any day.

Besides thorough cleaning and taking all possible steps to create peace in the home, your best tactics are close supervision, spending time alone with them and perhaps a confidence-building training class to reassure them that they still have a valued place in your heart and home. It can also be useful to spend time with them, just hanging out in the areas and on the furniture they used to mark so they are seen more as den space than toilet area.

For male dogs that mark, it will take about one week of strict supervision for every month your dog has been doing this behaviour to get it turned around. During that time, you will need to limit your

Potty Profile

dog's exposure to females in season. You may also need to limit his interactions with other male dogs, especially if he is inclined to be fractious or competitive.

The usual advice is to neuter, but it isn't quite the panacea that it's supposed to be. There can be a lot of good reasons to delay neutering or not neuter at all. While neutering can be helpful in reducing indoor marking, the most current research clearly shows that it can increase other problem behaviours. Most importantly, if your dog is inclined towards anxiety, neutering can make it worse—which can then lead to more marking. If you live somewhere that chemical neutering is available, it's well worth a short-term trial to see if any behaviour issues arise before committing to a non-reversible surgery.

There are also sound orthopaedic reasons for not neutering or delaying neutering. Delayed growth plate closure and increased risk of cruciate ligament injury are the most common concerns. Decisions need to be made on a case-by-case basis, and your decision should be informed by your own research, your individual dog's temperament, your breeder or breed club's recommendations and your veterinarian. This is another topic where an unbelievable amount of pressure is often heaped on dog owners, and I would like to gently remind you that this is *your* dog and therefore the decision is yours.

There are a couple extra steps you need to effectively deal with marking and leg-lifting. Cleaning is particularly important and is covered in detail in Chapter 12. If your dog has been marking for any significant amount of time, seriously consider investing in a portable fluorescent black light (my favourite has always been a small aquarium light and a long extension cord) to look for all the places you may need to clean. Apologies in advance for exposing you to the full horror of what you might find.

Housetraining That Works

In situations where you may not be able to supervise effectively, you may find it useful to have your male dog wear a "cummerbund" or belly band. These washable wraps are fairly easy to find on-line, and, although some dedicated dogs will choose to wet themselves consistently, most figure out quickly that they would be better served to just hold it until you remove it for potty runs.

Normally, belly bands are indoor attire but Taliesin was too embarrassed to pose in front of the girls. He would like you to know that this belly band isn't his. He is modelling it for a hairy friend who couldn't get a grooming appointment in time for picture day.

There are some "supporting behaviours" that tend to go along with indoor marking, and it can be helpful to eliminate as many as possible. Dogs that pee on every possible vertical object outside don't necessarily lift their leg inside, but every indoor leg-lifter I've ever met has been a seriously committed outdoor marker too. You would be well-served not to allow more than two or three pees on your walks.

Potty Profile

If your dog has marked on people or other dogs, train yourself to park your dog between your legs, or beside you in a sit or down position, if you stop to chat. Keep your leash very short until you get moving again. Avoid situations where your dog will be off leash around people standing still. Much as I lean heavily toward positive techniques, this is one of the few behaviours that I will interrupt with a sharp, "Oi!" or clap my hands if I see that telltale sidle. Anxiety probably plays a big part in this behaviour, but it's also just plain rude, even by dog standards.

Other supporting behaviours include elaborate or extravagant marking styles. Dogs that back themselves up to their targets and do handstands just to get a little extra height are at very high risk to offend. In male dogs, kicking after peeing or pooping also tends to indicate either an inappropriately inflated status or anxiety or both.* All these should be gently discouraged.

Last on my list is early onset leg-lifting. Some dogs wait until almost a year to leg-lift, and others never quite master it. Others will be inspired by a mentor showing them how it's done, and there are a few child prodigies who will confidently cock a leg even before teething starts in earnest. Gently but firmly discourage this by nudging or leaning to shift their weight back onto all four feet until they are at least six months old. Take my word for it that pups who strut their stuff extra early tend to have an attitude to match. These are the dogs who need the most structure and guidance and the least amount of freedom and unsupervised time.

---

*In female dogs, the behaviour seems to have a more gleeful, just-in-case-you-hadn't-noticed-my-awesomeness/hold-my-beer vibe.

Housetraining That Works

MY DOG'S REASONS FOR ACCIDENTS ARE:

☐ Age

☐ Medical conditions

☐ Nutrition/supplements

☐ Background

☐ Not clear where to go (or not go)

☐ Inside too long

☐ Doesn't know how to tell me they need out

☐ Fear / anxiety

☐ Submissive urination

☐ Marking or leg-lifting

TO TRAIN MY DOG I WILL NEED TO COMPLETE STEPS:

☑ #1 Complete a Potty Profile

☐ #2 Eliminate any medical or nutritional issues

☐ #3 Choose and set up safe potty and confinement issues

☐ #4 Train my dog to potty on cue and on leash

☐ #5 Create a Personal Potty Plan

Potty Profile

☐ **#6 Build Control**

☐ **#7 Learn a Signal**

In addition, I may need to... (use this space to note any extra accommodations—like taking an elderly dog out more frequently or using earplugs in fireworks season):

_____

_____

_____

_____

_____

_____

_____

_____

_____

_____

_____

_____

CHAPTER 5

Setting Up Your Potty Area

The first thing you have to do is choose the training model you're going to use. There are four options:

1. Outdoors
2. Indoor/outdoor combo
3. Indoors to start/outdoors eventually (or seasonally)
4. Indoors permanently

Outdoors

This is a great option if you live somewhere with reasonable weather and your dog is suited to your local climate, geography and incidence of predators. You also will need easy access to an outdoor space suitable for use as a permanent dog toilet area. For an average-sized dog living in an average climate, this is an ideal choice.

Housetraining That Works

Indoor/Outdoor Combo

This is the best choice when we have a puppy, a senior dog or a dog recovering from illness or surgery, and we need to be away some of the time. (I've even been told that some people aren't allowed to take their dogs to work!)

In this model, we might have the puppy use a crate as a den/sleeping area and take them outside as needed when we're home. When the puppy has to be left alone for longer than they can be crated, then the crate would be within a pen or other safe, confined space. The door to the crate gets removed or secured so puppy doesn't accidentally get shut in or out of their cozy place. If the puppy wakes up and they really have to go, they can step outside of their den and pee on something appropriate like a litter box or a pee pad. In the early stages it doesn't even matter if they miss the pad and most of it ends up on the floor—the behaviour we're establishing is *leaving the den to go potty*. Accuracy comes later.

This system actually works rather well. It allows the puppy some time to grow up a little and develop some control. When they get a little older and you know their toileting habits, it may be possible to crate them in the morning, pop home on a break (or arrange for a friend or dog-sitter) to check them and take them outside, and then use the pen for the rest of the day. Or the other way around.

Later, they can gradually transition to being a dog who goes exclusively outdoors. You just have to wait for them to develop enough bladder and bowel control for them to be consistently able to keep their crate clean without discomfort. Don't rush them—it is seriously unpleasant to come home to a dog who has pooped in their crate. (And it's very distressing for your dog too.)

Setting Up Your Potty Area

Indoors to Start/Outdoors Eventually (or Seasonally)

Back when dinosaurs roamed the earth, this was how everybody housetrained their dog. You covered your kitchen or bathroom in newspaper, let the dog go wherever and whenever they wanted within that space and then, over the course of several weeks or months, gradually reduced the space that was papered.

Eventually, there was one tiny postage stamp of paper which you were then supposed to drag out your back door to the yard and pray your dog got the idea. (All the dog training books of the day had cautionary notes about how careful one had to be about leaving newspapers laying around if you didn't want them peed on!)

This approach has largely fallen out of favour, but, with a few modifications, it can be useful in a lot of situations.

You might have a tiny little dog or a very young pup and not want to risk taking them outside. Perhaps you live somewhere really cold and you don't want to lose your dog in a snow bank. You might live in a really tall apartment building and not like your chances of getting your puppy leashed, collared, into the elevator, all the way downstairs and around the corner to the only available strip of grass before their bladder lets go.

There can be medical reasons (yours or your dog's) why outside isn't ideal just yet. Or you could be a caregiver for an elderly parent or a baby and not be able to juggle meeting their needs and getting outside. And sometimes outside just isn't safe.

Starting indoors and moving outdoors can take a little longer and might need more patience, but it's a perfectly valid option. If going outside consistently just isn't available right now, it's perfectly all right to give your dog an indoor toilet area. Just keep in mind that we want to transition to outdoors eventually (or possibly just seasonally).

Indoors Permanently

This is my least favourite model, but there are times when it's the best choice. In some areas of the world, dogs who live in really dense urban settings just don't ever go outside. If you have mobility challenges or are otherwise differently able, outside may just not be possible. Or you might live in an area with serious predators.

At the time of this writing, we share our home with three medium-to-large-sized dogs and a four-pounds-when-soaking-wet Yorkshire Terrier. We live in an area that has a lot of eagles, bobcats and cougars. (Makes a nice change from the bears at our last place!) We also have nesting great horned owls on our property. To survive her evening potty runs, our tiny tyke does not go out without a flashing light collar and another dog trained to look for aerial predators.

It would be a perfectly reasonable thing for our tiny little "cat snack" of a dog to just have an indoor potty area. The main reason we don't is because we have larger dogs (and sometimes guest dogs) as well, and I don't want them getting the idea that they can go inside too.

If you're going to make your dog a permanent indoor pottier, make your life easier and set up their toilet area in your bathroom. It's just a lot easier and cleaner and less off-putting for guests than having a dog toilet right in your living room or in your entryway.

Treat their toilet area as if it were a backyard and follow all the same protocols about going on leash and on cue. Otherwise, you run the risk of having a dog with almost no bladder control, and then you'll

Setting Up Your Potty Area

never go to the bathroom alone again because you won't be able to risk closing the door!

My Dog's Housetraining Model Will Be:

☐ Outdoors

☐ Indoor/outdoor combo

☐ Indoors to start/outdoors eventually (or seasonally)

☐ Indoors permanently

Choose a Location

Your next task is to choose a suitable location. Whether your dog will have an indoor or an outdoor toilet area, it needs to be easy to find, safe and appealing. While the idea of a dog toilet near your house might not fill you with joy, please don't be tempted to locate their bathroom out the front door, around the side of the house, down to the very back of the back yard, tucked in behind the shed next to the neighbour's pet hellhound who's snarling through the fence and saying mean things about how edible your dog looks.

Ideally, their potty spot should be in a straight line from wherever your dog exits the house or their confinement space. It should be the shortest distance possible from the house and, in a perfect world, visible from the door. You need to be able to get your puppy to their destination as quickly as possible.

Once they're confident and reliable about going to that spot and using it, you'll be able to hang back a bit and let them go ahead.

Housetraining That Works

Eventually, you won't have to go with them every time. You'll be able to stand in the doorway drinking coffee while your lovely dog braves the elements. Being able to see them from where you stand allows you to praise them lavishly for a job well done. Choosing your location wisely pays off big time.

Choosing indoor locations is a little trickier. If you plan to transition your dog to going outside within 3-6 months, your potty area in the house is probably going to be somewhere that you wouldn't choose for a *permanent* indoor location. You want it to be as close to the exit door as possible because, even if they have to use an indoor bathroom for now, they need to get in the habit of heading towards the exit door when they need to go. If the exit door for the future *outdoor* potty area is in one direction and their *indoor* bathroom space is in the other direction, you're going to have a much harder time transitioning them when the time comes.

For example, if you plan to use a space in the back yard, and your back yard is accessed through the kitchen, sometimes that means you have an x-pen or gates confining your dog to the kitchen. Inevitably, there will be some accidents, which is kind of yucky for a food preparation area, but this is *short term*.

Selecting a permanent indoor area is a little easier—mostly because your options are pretty limited. Carpeted areas, high traffic areas, living rooms, home offices, dens, bedrooms and dining areas are obviously off the list. Usually, that leaves you with bathroom, laundry room or hallway.

If you are lucky enough to have an attached carport, garage or even a balcony, these should move to the top of your list. They have the added benefit of being outside your actual living space so your dog will have to learn to hold it at least long enough to tell you they need to go out.

Setting Up Your Potty Area

The next best choice is the bathroom. If we're going to have pee in the house, let it be in the same place that everybody else goes for that. In addition to being easy to clean, your dog won't take long to figure out that their whole human pack uses the space for the same purpose. That can be very reinforcing and may speed up the process.

One exception to this otherwise ideal location is if your bathroom is carpeted. Don't even consider sabotaging your dog's progress with this weirdest of decor choices. (Stop! Don't tell me why yours is okay—that's a clear cry for help and you should probably see a professional.) The fact that dogs really like them tells you everything you need to know about why we'll be choosing somewhere else. You'll thank me the first time your dog gets the runs.

A laundry room can be another good choice, provided it's close to where the dog spends the most time. Perhaps not the best for noise-sensitive dogs, and care must be taken to stow any toxic products securely and out of reach. With puppies, you also have to be careful about leaving tempting clothing items dangling.

NB: Whatever your final choice, please don't make the dog go down a gazillion stairs to the creepy basement just to go to the bathroom.

Cautionary Notes:

When dogs have indoor potty areas, it's best not to give them constant access during the training process because every time they have the faintest inkling they'd like to potty, they'll run to their spot for instant relief—no waiting—and they really don't develop bladder and bowel control. They also don't learn to go on cue and with you watching, which can be problematic when they go with you somewhere new. Treat your indoor potty space like it's the great outdoors and take them to it on leash at the same intervals as you would for going outside. There's plenty of time later to allow them the run of the house.

The same thing can happen with dog doors or doors left open to the back yard. Every fall when the weather turns cold or wet, my phone will start ringing about that perfect springtime puppy who was always so good and "housetrained themselves" and is now having accidents by the door. Set yourself up for success: be careful about your choice of location and mindful of the long-term effects for the access you're allowing.

Make It Safe

Earlier, we talked a bit about how the potty area has to not only *be* safe, it has to *feel* safe too. For both of you. You're probably already clear about what makes you feel safe and comfortable (no one in a clown costume holding a machete, well lit, no varmints or vermin, no sharp obstacles or tripping hazards, no weird sounds, no really awful smells and absolutely no inter-galactic portals) but dogs and humans have different ideas on what that means. Your dog's list of hazards and threats—real or imagined—will have some crossover with yours. Unless you have an Irish Setter, machete-wielding clowns are likely on both your lists. Same for most of the predators. You will likely disagree on some of the vermin (aka desirable snacks/playthings) and most of the smells. They don't usually mind the inter-galactic portals, but the neighbour's creepy, staring cat definitely has mob connections.

If your dog is extremely shy or frightened about going to the bathroom in front of you, it may be necessary to set up a visual barrier where you're sort of behind a screen or a tree.

(Which gets a little tricky because you're trying to do this on leash.)

Setting Up Your Potty Area

Something that rarely gets mentioned is just how many dogs fear the dark. Going out at night can be really scary for them, so please make sure it's well lit at night. A big clue is if your dog's first housetraining accidents happened right after the clocks changed or you noticed an outdoor lightbulb needing to be replaced.

If you have a noise-sensitive dog, and there's a rock band playing in the garage next door, they're not likely to feel safe or relaxed enough to potty (your dog, not the band—rock musicians are not known for being shy about these things). Same goes for roadwork, construction or neighbours who scream at each other a lot. Your options for locations might be limited, but do your best to create a haven of calm. If your dog will accept them, earplugs may help.

Strange, loud or new sounds may be experienced as exciting, distracting or terrifying. Watch your dog carefully and try to observe the world through their senses. Some fears will fade with maturity and experience, but others may linger without behavioural intervention. Proceed with compassion.

Make It Sexy

Remember, we're trying to create an executive bathroom experience for your dog—a toilet area so appealing that going anywhere else is a bit of a letdown. There are three main things on your dog's wish list for the perfect bathroom: cleanliness, level of exclusivity and tactile preference.

First, and most important, is cleanliness. The vast majority of dogs much prefer to be clean and will tend to go poop at least a couple body lengths away from the last place they went. Please don't fall into the trap of "leaving some there to give them the idea"—that can go from helpfully suggestive to irredeemably aversive pretty darn quick. I've never met a dog who enjoyed tip-toeing through a minefield of old poops.

Think about what it's like when you go somewhere where there's a row of bathroom stalls. If the first toilet is disgusting, you might not just skip the next one but instead go two or three doors down. Nobody wants to be anywhere near that. If the next one's a mess, then you're likely to go even further. Sometimes you're forced to go to the one clean stall between two dirty stalls. It's gross and you don't usually go back to that place if you can avoid it. If that were a movie theatre or a restaurant, you'd be complaining to the manager, but your dog can't do that. They can only speak to us through their behavior. So keep it clean.

Next up is the level of exclusivity. That is, understanding whether your dog is a "party pooper" or a little more introverted. In much the same way that some people seem to love hanging out in the bathrooms at the mall and chatting while they're on the throne, some dogs like a bathroom that is frequented by others. Wherever dogs hang out, there's always a favourite tree or rock or fencepost where all the cool dogs go. Shyer dogs may want more of a "fortress of solitude" experience and find multi-dog potty areas quite intimidating. If you have a yard, this isn't an issue but if you're having to take your dog out on the street, it's worth knowing if your dog would prefer a less popular rock, tree or patch of grass.

Many dogs appreciate a little bit of privacy. For some, it's not so much about the privacy as it is about making sure that no human sees them going to the bathroom because that's been bad news for them in the past. You will soon be a master of the minor but very useful superpower called "watching your dog closely while appearing to be doing nothing of the sort." Humming vaguely, turning away

Setting Up Your Potty Area

slightly and occasionally glancing at the sky to check for rain are good first steps.

Last on the list for the perfect dog bathroom is tactile preference. That is, the thing they're used to feeling under their feet when they go to the bathroom. Most dogs have a preference—to the point where it can actually trigger the need to go, and standing on anything else may inhibit them. Which is great if you have a back yard and they're used to grass but not so much fun if you have wall-to-wall carpet and they were raised on towels. That's why it really helps to know what your dog used for a bathroom in its prior home.

If your dog spent time in a shelter, you might want to ask if they pooped in their indoor area or held it until they got outside. If they were given a blanket, did they sleep on it or just shove it into a corner and pee on it because they have a tactile preference for fabric?

If you have a shiny new puppy, you'll need to know what they were raised on. What was in the den area, and what was right outside the den area? What surface did they actually use for a bathroom?

Breeders often use pea gravel (sorry, pun intended), wood chips or wood pellets for their dog toileting areas. Others raise theirs on concrete runs but have a grassy area. If you have a light coloured or white-coated dog from a show breeder, please know that they are sometimes raised on white paper. It's easy to keep clean and doesn't stain the coats. If you share my dinosaur tendencies and still enjoy print media, you will need to be vigilant about leaving newspaper sections laying about.

Dogs who have been trained on pee pads will usually have a tactile preference for fabric because that's what it feels like under their feet. If you want to transition them to using grass, you may have to be a bit clever. A good first step is to put a pee pad out on the grass in the potty area and weigh it down with a couple of rocks. Give them a few days to get comfy using the pad in its new outdoor location. Then, over time, just cut little pieces off it or put a piece of sod over one corner of it until gradually it's covered. Ta-dah! You've successfully transitioned your dog to a new tactile surface.

If you're lucky, what your dog prefers is what you have available. If you live somewhere with back yards, it's usually grass. If you live in a major urban centre, it's really helpful to have a dog who is comfortable going to the bathroom on concrete.

It's also important to acknowledge your own preferences. For instance, I'm not a fan of dogs that prefer concrete because poop on sidewalks is pretty disgusting. Have you ever been walking down a sidewalk and suddenly your dog is pooping and everyone's staring at you? Not my favourite experience. What's even worse is that my own dogs prefer grass or getting into the woods, so I'm not expecting it and may not even have a poop bag. Trying to scoop a poop into someone else's discarded coffee cup is not on my list of favourite activities!

Note: If you plan to travel with your dog, you may want to get them comfortable on multiple surfaces. There's not always a grassy area or spare set of woods nearby.

My Dog's Executive Bathroom:

☐ **Is easy to get to**

☐ **Is safe**

☐ **Feels safe (for me and my dog)**

Setting Up Your Potty Area

☐ **Has a "just right" level of exclusivity**

☐ **Has an appealing surface**

> **Important Housetraining Shortcut:**
>
> **Did you know that the Housetraining Fairy will grant you 50% faster housetraining if you promise to never knowingly let your dog pee on a fire hydrant? It's true! Even if you don't believe me, firefighters do enough for us without having to deal with a couple hundred layers of dried dog urine every time they open a hydrant. Plus, the urine corrodes them. Seriously, no peeing on hydrants— not even the ones that get installed at dog parks as a joke. Don't be a jerk.**

CHAPTER 6

Setting Up Confinement Areas

Why do we need a confinement area? Well, we can't supervise them all the time—sometimes we need our own potty breaks. Yes, I know you can take them with you when they're little, but don't even try to go pee in the company of a friendly six-month-old Great Dane puppy. Unless you're living a really ideal life where you have no distractions, and your puppy can be with you or carried around by you at all times, you're going to have some times when your dog has to be confined. Ideally, that confinement will keep them safe and limit their options for mayhem when you can't supervise directly.

Once again, choose your model. Your options are:

1. Pretending this doesn't apply to you because your brand-new puppy is perfect and never leaves your side. Your local carpet and flooring store would like to thank you in advance for sending their kids to college.

2. Crate training for nighttime, naps and the occasional short stretch of time alone. You will need to use a house leash

to keep your pup within sight when not in their crate. Works well for older dogs or if you spend most of your day outdoors, but if you have a brand-new pup and ever have to actually get something done, you may need to look for a more flexible solution.

3. One gated-off room like a small kitchen or study. (Also works well in RVs or if you live on a boat.) Can work really well if that's where you spend most of your time or if you've been thinking about replacing your kitchen cupboards. Your contractor and local home supply store also like this option.

4. An x-pen or crate/x-pen combo. Pretty much the perfect solution.

5. A dog run. Can be useful but not ideal. More on that later.

6. Tossing them out in the back yard when you can't directly supervise and hoping they don't learn to dig, destroy your patio furniture, escape or eat a toxic plant and need to go to the vet. Your veterinarian is looking forward to paying off their mortgage early.

There is no seventh option because you will not be chaining your dog. Yes, I know there are a few situations where this is appropriate—sled dogs being picketed between runs or hunting dogs waiting their turn at a field trial, for instance. It is a rare dog who can handle being chained without developing serious behaviour issues. Generally speaking, chained dogs never come in the house and are NOT HOUSETRAINED. Keep that in mind if you've just adopted one.

Setting Up Confinement Areas

Note: It's totally okay to choose more than one option—just not 1 or 6.

Let's take a closer look at options 2–5:

Crates

Crating is a marvellous option for dogs who have been properly introduced to them, but they do have some limitations. If your dog is an adult from an awesome breeder, shelter or rescue, then they are probably already comfortable sleeping in a crate at night and taking naps during the day. Look no further—you have found the perfect confinement option. If, on the other hand, your dog has never been in a crate or has had a bad crate experience, it may be a while before crating is a viable option.

If you've just brought home an eight-week-old puppy, they can really only be left in that crate for brief periods during the day—at least for the first little while. You'll need a more flexible option and a bit more space if you need to take the kids to school or go grocery shopping.

Nevertheless, crating should be seen as a nearly essential skill with applications far beyond housetraining. Getting your dog used to one is a top priority. Whether for safe car travel, sanctuary from visiting toddlers, emergency evacuations, staying with friends or extended veterinary care, it's very likely that at some point in your dog's life, you will be very grateful that you taught them how to cope with confinement.

Stick with either molded plastic or wire crates. I'm not as big a fan of the wire crates. They're heavy, can be surprisingly fiddly to clean, tend to corrode at the joints and they have too many pinch points.

Also, dogs manage to wiggle out of them in the weirdest ways. I only use them for dogs that need help staying cool because they have better airflow.

Your dog may graduate to a lightweight fabric crate when they're older, but please don't use one for housetraining puppies because they'll eat or claw their way out. Fabric crates are also difficult to clean.

Crate Size and Features

Be sure to choose an appropriately sized crate for your dog. They should be able to stand or sit without their ears touching the top, and they need to be able to turn around and lay down comfortably. Take into consideration whether your dog is a curler or a sprawler when sleeping, but please don't buy something two sizes too big because you feel guilty. Tell your primate brain to back off and give your dog the cozy den they need.

With puppies, there is always a temptation to buy a crate large enough for their adult self, but please consider borrowing or buying one that's suitable for your pup's current size. Yes, it's a pain to keep sizing up, but if you buy second hand you can usually re-sell for what you paid for them.

Some crates have an optional divider that can be taken out as the pup grows. Otherwise, if the crate is too big, they will sleep at one end and use the other for a bathroom—and they'll be really happy to share that mess with you when you get home. So, unless you want "poo polka dot" to be your new signature look, keep your dog's crate appropriately den sized.

Setting Up Confinement Areas

One feature worth looking for is a door that has two latches and opens either way. Very handy when you move the crate to a location that makes one side awkward or if not everyone in the house has the same dominant hand. The best part is that you can easily remove the door entirely without having to unscrew all those little bolts to clean the crate after a poo disaster.

Safety Considerations:

Dogs in crates must be naked. Puppies even more so. That means no collars, no leashes, no nothing. Especially if you're not home. Puppies are very talented at finding ways to strangle themselves, and no one should have to come home and face that. It's just too awful. Even if you're home with them, if they get their tag or collar caught in the door and they panic, they can strangle while you're still trying to figure out how to get the door open.

Also, unless your pup is going on a plane, remove the stupid plastic water dish before your dog eats it and has to go to the vet. Replace it with a small stainless-steel bucket or dish that clips to the crate door.

Tethering

One of the easiest and most effective ways to supervise or confine a dog during housetraining is to use a "house leash" to tether them to you—or to something solid near you. You can sit and read a book, putter around the house, catch up on desk work—all while still keeping a close eye on your dog. Unless you're dealing with a very young pup or a leg-lifter, they are much less likely to go to the bathroom if they're right beside you. Also, your dog is much more likely to communicate that they need to go out, and you are much more likely to notice subtle signals.

Housetraining That Works

A house leash needn't be fancy. Don't spend a lot of money on something that your puppy will invariably chew. Save the adorable rainbow pawprint-patterned leash and collar matched sets for going on walks. Get yourself a couple cheap dollar store leashes or just buy a reel of utility cord (not too heavy and definitely not the nasty yellow stuff that rips your hands) and some leash snaps and make a bunch of leashes in lengths from six to ten feet. You might even make some of the longer outdoor versions called "draglines." At some point, your dog is going to drag their house leash or dragline through something really nasty, and it's nice to just be able to bin it because it wasn't expensive and you have a replacement on hand.

If you have limited space, equipment or budget, tethering to you is a really great way to go.

Sneaky Trainer Bonus Behaviour Hack:

House leashes and drag lines are my all-time favourite dog training tools. My puppies are on leash almost full time for the first nine to twelve months, whether they're indoors or outdoors. Sometimes they're tied to me and sometimes they're just dragging their leash—depending on the level of distraction or potential for disaster. The only time that line comes off is when they're in their crate or a very secure area. Same goes for adult dogs who are new to me.

In addition to housetraining, using house leashes and drag lines accelerates all training programs by preventing unwanted behaviours. It's easy to teach "tradesies" when they pick up something that isn't theirs if diving under the bed with the item isn't an option. It's simple to prevent jumping up by just stepping on their leash and rewarding them for staying down. Teething and mouthing are far more manageable when you have a way to hold them away from your pant leg until they're willing to consider a more acceptable chew toy.

Setting Up Confinement Areas

Developing a reliable recall goes a lot faster if the pup hasn't learned how much fun it is to run off and trigger an unscheduled game of tag. Learning to "stay" is much easier for a dog to grasp if leaving you without your permission has never been possible in the first place. By far, though, the most important benefit of all is the quality and strength of the relationship you'll build by rewarding what you want rather than allowing mistakes and then scolding them.

Safety Considerations:

If you're a little unsteady on your feet and your dog is of the "non-linear" and bouncy variety, be careful not to get hog-tied or trip over them. Consider tethering to something near you instead. Doors are an excellent choice—especially if you run the tether under the door from the knob on the opposite side.

Please be sure that whatever object you choose will not transform into a dog-chasing monster. Once you've seen a panic-stricken dog racing down a busy street with a metal plant stand in hot pursuit, you tend to be a little sceptical about any given object's ability to stay put. Table legs are also surprisingly easy to remove. So much fun when the tabletop is glass. Go ahead—ask me how I know. Also, can we just agree now that tethering a dog to a baby stroller is a really stupid idea? (I started to run as soon as I saw the mum step away from the stroller but wasn't fast enough, and I never want to see that again.)

Exercise Pens

"X-pens" are those folding wire enclosures that are made of connected panels. You can configure them in just about any shape you like, expand them by attaching additional panels and set them up anywhere you like in a matter of minutes. You can also combine them with a cozy crate, and they come in a variety of heights. These are the ideal choice if you have to be away from your pup longer than they can nap in their crate or if you have an open floor plan. Dogs who haven't been crate trained yet usually find x-pens easier to accept.

NB: If you have small children, an x-pen is *essential*—dogs and kids both need clear boundaries, safe spaces and quiet times.

Sneaky Trainer Bonus Behaviour #1: "Four on the Floor"

The reason dogs jump up is that it often gets them what they want, it gets them closer to you and it gets them looked at, spoken to and touched. It doesn't matter to them that you're looking at them crossly, scolding them and pushing them away—they want your attention, and they'll take it any way they can get it.

If you're using an x-pen, you can control what behaviours get reinforced. Train yourself to always pet your dog through the lower bars rather than reaching over the top, to give all treats down low and to never open the pen until all four paws are responding to gravity.

If your pup jumps up on the pen as you approach, stop in your tracks and pretend you've forgotten what you were about to do. Resume your approach when their feet hit the floor, then stop and stare at the ceiling when they jump up again. Don't be discouraged—the first time you try this, it will take several attempts. It gets easier quickly.

If your timing is good, you can even say, "Yes!" when they get it right. You can reward with small treats, but it's important to recognize that you moving closer is also reinforcing. Make sure your friends and

Setting Up Confinement Areas

family also know that pups on two legs are invisible but puppies with feet on the ground get all the goodies.

Your dog will soon realize that humans are easily distracted from simple tasks, and the easiest way to get us to come when we're called is to keep their feet on the ground and maintain eye contact lest we wander off. When they do, it's perfectly okay to quietly say, "Four on the floor" or "Gravity works!" if you'd like to put this behaviour on a verbal cue. It's also okay to say nothing and just let your stillness be their cue to consider a lower elevation.

If your dog is very young or has some experience in owner training, they may even offer you a sit. Feel free to name it when you see it, but please don't stand outside the pen repeating the word while your dog is leaping about lest you accidentally teach your dog that word means they should jump up.

Safety Considerations:

Just like with crates, they have to be naked when they're in the x-pen. All collars, leashes and harnesses have to come off. They cannot wear those things when they're confined and especially not when they're confined and left alone.

Never underestimate your dog's desire to climb. Choose an x-pen that is at least a foot taller than the height of your dog's estimated adult size. Preferably more. Don't just think you can get a taller one if they learn to climb. If they manage to "summit" a two-footer, the three-foot model will just be an appealing challenge. They'll climb that, and the four-footer will meet the same fate. Just get the tall one to start with.

Consider adding a lid. Sometimes you can buy them but they'll only fit if you form your pen into a square, and that might not work for your space. Also, your local pet store might not carry them. In that case, you can make a simple lid using zip ties and a piece of fence wire.

Just in case this isn't clear enough, you must discourage climbing. Falling from a height can seriously injure or kill a dog (the little ones are especially fragile). Dogs sometimes catch a leg and get stuck on the way down. Not a fun way for them to spend the afternoon if you're away.

Another issue is that some puppies will throw themselves at the sides of the pen and make it travel across your floor. That doesn't seem like a big deal until the pen that you left on the nice, easy-to-clean kitchen linoleum finds its way onto the living room carpet.

The other variation is that as they continue to throw themselves against that nice square x-pen, it morphs into a narrow rectangle. If it gets flattened enough, it can fall over and allow your puppy to escape or, even worse, trap your puppy between the panels. You don't want to come home and find your puppy has been rampaging around your house unsupervised for hours or that they've been injured by a falling x-pen.

If the x-pen is only going to be used when you're nearby, you needn't worry, but if your dog will be alone for any period of time, you will need to take steps to avoid disaster. Some dogs are particularly talented at finding ways to injure themselves or wreak havoc, and you really don't want to find out yours is the evil genius of the litter.

Prevention is fairly simple—attaching a turnbuckle in each corner will help maintain the shape and stability. Some people use spring clamps or a few inches of PVC with a slot cut along the length. (See illustration for examples.) Now just anchor it to something so that it can't travel, determine whether you need a lid and you're all set.

Setting Up Confinement Areas

Your turnbuckle does not need to be this large. A 4-6" long one at each corner will effectively prevent x-pen collapse.

There's all sorts of ways to secure the joints of an x-pen. This is my favourite. It's just a short section of scrap PVC pipe with a cut running the length of it.

Housetraining That Works

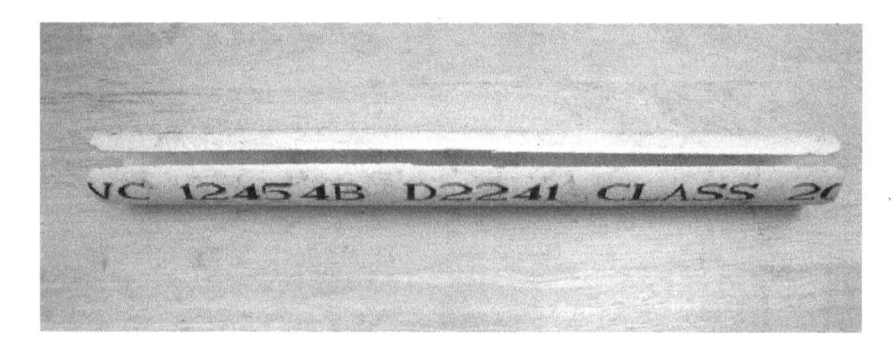

PVC pipe showing the cut on the underside.

NB: If you're doing a crate/x-pen combination, make sure you secure your dog's crate door in the open position or remove it entirely. You also need to assess whether your dog is likely to see the crate as a cozy sleep space or a steppingstone to freedom. Some dogs were goats in a previous life.

Crate with door securely in open position. I recommend using a dollar store chain leash rather than something expensive and chewable like this fancy leather one.

Setting Up Confinement Areas

One Small Room

Those of us who have lived on boats or in small cabins will tend to gravitate to this option. Ditto RVs. This strategy works best if the room they're gated in also has you in it most of the time. For instance, I wrote a lot of this book in my office with a gate across the door and a puppy at my feet, and I wrote a bunch more at the kitchen table—my "morning office," again with attached puppy.

This is also a good option if you have a very large puppy or dog. Even if you can find a suitable crate for a Great Dane, the size may not work in the space you have available. Just be aware that your dog may not differentiate between "appropriate chew toy" and "furniture" without consistent guidance. Also, just because they don't have thumbs doesn't mean they can't open cupboards. The likelihood of your dog getting into something that requires veterinary care is directly correlated to how much you can't afford it right now.

Try to avoid confining a dog to a laundry room or bathroom unless you spend a lot of time in them or there's a good view of the more popular parts of the home. Dogs are social animals, and there's a big difference between coping with a little alone time and being isolated. If you have to use a more isolated space, try to confine its use to when you're not home. Use a crate, x-pen or tethering when you're home.

Dog Runs

These are best avoided for young dogs. It's way too easy for them to learn to just poop anywhere, anytime and never develop the control needed to join the household. Most dogs quickly get bored and start racing back and forth barking their fool heads off. Your neighbours will love that.

There's a time and a place for dog runs, but I don't think house training is that time. If you must use one, please limit the hours they spend there and make sure they have protection from heat, cold, rain and wind.

Safety Considerations:

Dogs left outside are at much higher risk of being stolen or poisoned. Please make sure you have clearly visible security cameras and lock your dog run even if you live in the middle of nowhere. It is beyond awful to come home and find your dog gone.

My dog's confinement and supervision strategies will be:

☐ **Crate**

☐ **Tethering to me or something solid near me**

☐ **Exercise pen**

☐ **One small room**

☐ **Dog run**

CHAPTER 7

Teaching Potty Cues

Why We Teach a Potty Cue

Now that you know *where* you want your dog to go to the bathroom, it's time to teach them to actually go *when* they're asked. Why is this important? Why can't we just take them outside, wait until they pee and give them a treat? Partly because you may not want to stand in your yard for half an hour while it's raining sideways and even more because sometimes there will be situations where you just need a way to tell your dog this is an okay place to go to the bathroom. Most importantly, you need to be able to reliably get them empty so you know when you can let them have a little unsupervised or less supervised time loose in your home.

Female vs. Male Dogs:

The only significant difference between female and male dogs as far as housetraining goes is that the girls can generally get by with one potty cue and will generalize that to mean "whatever you need to do, do it now," whether it's pee or poop. Boy dogs will quite often need a second cue. Otherwise, when you tell him to "get busy," he'll just go pee. If you're pretty sure he's got to poop as well and cue him again, he'll pee again. And again. Depending on the dog, he might keep this up until you could submit his bladder as evidence for an alternate dimension.* So I find it really helpful for male dogs to have a second command that is specifically for bowel movements.

While we're on the subject of marking, promise me now that you will not allow your dog to pee on corners of buildings, entryways to stores or apartments, people, trail markers, park entries, playground equipment, fire hydrants, mailboxes, tires, park benches, public art displays, or the first object that catches their fancy after passing another dog. Let's go even further and make human-made objects off-limits, wherever possible.

Besides just smelling awful, there can be behavioural fall-out for excessive marking. Sometimes, allowing a dog to claim a high-value territory can create anxiety about potentially having to defend it.

If you really believe your dog's happiness depends on anointing stuff, take them on dedicated pee walks and give them permission. (We say, "Fill your boots" when my husband takes our boy for their evening male-bonding stroll.) The rest of the time, get them empty at the start and then just go for your walk. One last pee just before they go back inside should satisfy everyone's requirements.

---

* It is completely unnecessary for male dogs to mark everything that strikes their fancy. When housetraining adult male dogs, allow one pee for the main event and one bonus pee to make sure they're empty. That's quite enough for cultural expression of masculinity. After they've peed twice, you should consider all marking to be three-foot-high graffiti of questionable artistic merit.

Teaching Potty Cues

Why We Teach This on Leash

Why can't you just shiver in your bathrobe by the back door? Because especially in the first two to four weeks of house training, it is critical that you curate the housetraining experience. Don't be tempted to just let your dog out in the backyard and hope for the best. Long term, that's a recipe for disaster.

When you first take a brand-new puppy outside, they'll sniff around a little bit, and they'll usually pee fairly promptly whether they're on-leash or off. The world is big, exciting and new wherever they are, and they hit overwhelm pretty quickly, so they usually don't mind going back inside.

When they get older, if you're still just letting them wander around outside having a grand old time until they go, they quickly learn to hold it longer and longer so they can keep having fun and destroying your yard. When you finally bring them back in because you realize you're late for work or you decide they must not need to go, they'll usually have an accident before you can pour your coffee or even hang up your coat.

Prevention is simple: teach your dog to go to the bathroom on cue, on leash, and reserve all fun until after they get the job done—then celebrate! Remember, "No potty, no party."

Important:

On-leash pottying isn't just for puppies. Sooner or later your dog will need to know how to do this. At some point your dog will face less than ideal travel conditions, areas that are unsafe for off-leash or veterinary care, and you will be very glad you taught them this essential skill.

Housetraining That Works

Also, there's a certain amount of trust needed to accomplish an on-leash potty run. A lot of dogs like a little privacy and distance for going to the bathroom. While it's nice to acknowledge and honour their wishes, they also just need to be comfortable enough with you to relax and get the job done.

This can be especially tricky for dogs with challenging backgrounds as they often don't want to draw attention to their bathroom habits. It's important for them to learn that it's okay to go to the bathroom on a leash in front of us. Learning that pottying actually gets rewarded can be a huge breakthrough.

Is On-Leash Pottying a Forever Thing?

Nope. It's a best practice until you've been accident free for a couple months thing. Going on cue is an awesome way to speed up housetraining. So is going on leash. Combining the two makes for warp-speed progress.

Eventually, you will reach the point where your dog does not need to be escorted and supervised for all bathroom excursions. There will come that one blissful morning where you stagger out of bed, open the back door and they go straight to their potty area while you clutch your morning coffee.

(Just remember to check every now and then that they still remember how to go on leash.)

Teaching Potty Cues

Choosing a Potty Cue

You can choose just about any word or phrase you like. Your dog does not have a dictionary and is unlikely to question your choice of "pickles and walnuts" as a potty cue, but it's a good idea to choose something that other people will be able to remember and understand.

Avoid anything that rhymes with other common cues lest you meet with disaster when asking your dog to "Sit"! Take my word for it that, if you have children, "Hurry up!" would be an ill-advised choice. Racehorses are commonly trained to pee on a whistle cue to facilitate rapid post-race drug tests, but that could cause problems if you plan to use a whistle to call your dog or you have a whistler in your house.

One last cautionary note—if anyone besides yourself will be taking the dog out, please don't use something they'd be embarrassed to say within earshot of the neighbours. This rule is dedicated to the very proper, very British, retired officer (he didn't actually wear a monocle, but I always remember him with one because he was so very David Niven) whose wife made him do all the after dark potty runs with their tiny little poodle. Their potty area was well within earshot of their neighbours, and the cue phrase she had trained in was "Make presents for mommy." Just don't.

My dogs are usually trained to rather dull cues like "Get busy" or "Do your stuff," but sometimes a "procrasti-pooper" will get trained to a rocket launch countdown. They're pretty clear that if "blast-off" does not occur by the time we get to zero, they'll be going back in their crate.

There's also fun to be had in creating potty cue songs by substituting words in popular songs. Yes, it's silly, but it's easier for dogs to relax and go to the bathroom if we're not sounding cross, and it's hard to sound cross when you're singing. I have several go-to ditties and would be happy to share, but copyright rules are scary, so you'll have to use your imagination.

How We Teach Potty Cues

For the first three to five days, when you take your dog out to potty, you're going to go straight to the bathroom area, and you are going to be seriously boring for two or three minutes. You're going to do your best impression of a tree. Nothing fun is going to happen. You're not going to be telling them to go to the bathroom or praising them for successfully breathing. Just stand still and zip it. Then you're going to wait until you see the behaviour you want.*

When you see a puppy start to pee or poop, you're going to start "layering" your cue over that behaviour. In your best imitation of a cooing pigeon, you will quietly repeat your cue for the duration of the event. When the peeing stops or the poo drops, stop saying your

---

* There will be times when you're sure your dog needs to potty and they just won't go. Trust your instincts—they need to go. The good news is you don't have to just stand around waiting indefinitely. If nothing happens in three to five minutes, it probably isn't going to happen. Take your pup back inside but return them to the smallest version of their confinement area immediately. Or carry them around if possible. Try again in five to fifteen minutes. If the next time is also unsuccessful, you can increase your intervals to thirty minutes. Remember, nothing fun happens until they go where you want them to go. We'll discuss Potty Run Protocols in greater detail in Chapter 8.

Teaching Potty Cues

cue word or phrase. Now you may reward your dog with something tasty or a play session.* Or both.

Your next step is to spend several days learning what behaviour your dog does in the split second *before* they pee or poop. When you can accurately predict when pottying is going to occur, start slipping in your verbal cues just before they go.

When you've had two weeks of at least 80% success predicting the behaviour and cueing at the appropriate time, you may begin taking them out to their potty area when you know they need to go and just telling them to go. You're welcome.

If at any time you notice that there's an increasing delay between when you tell them to go and when they actually go, you may need to backtrack to being quiet and slipping your cue in at the right time so you don't accidentally train in "getting ready to potty" instead of actually going.

Peeing is pretty easy to get on cue—mostly because they do it more often so there are more opportunities to reward the behaviour. Pooping on cue is a little trickier. There are more precursor behaviours, so be extra careful about your timing. Do not start saying your cue

---

* Some dogs appreciate warm praise at this point, but shyer dogs or those with tricky histories might be alarmed by that level of attention paid to them in close proximity to pee or poop. Instead, let their reward be allowing them to exit the situation.

These dogs often benefit from a few days of you being silent (no cue words) and not looking at them directly until they've after they've gone to the bathroom. Hold off on adding a cue until they are comfortable going to the bathroom in front of you on leash. There are enough environmental and physiological prompts to get the party started—you can add the verbal cues later.

before you're absolutely certain that the main event is actually going to happen. It is irritatingly easy to accidentally train your dog to do all the behaviours *leading up to* pooping—to the point where the cue will actually prevent them from going. Signs might include sniffing, circling, squatting, a bulging rectum or just giving you pointed looks because they want some distance and privacy.

Reinforcing Pottying on Cue

In the short term we're going to reward them with an actual yummy something. The harder it is for your dog to go to the bathroom in front of you, the higher value the treat should be. Be sure to "read the room" —some dogs really appreciate their post-potty payoff while others will give you such a look.

After a week or two, begin to fade the treats for peeing and only occasionally offer one, almost as an afterthought. Continue to reward for pooping outside until you have had at least two weeks of no accidents in the house and you're not having any difficulty getting them to poop in your view. In the long run, the reward for going to the bathroom when they're told to is that they get relief.

Note: If your dog is prone to coprophagy (eating poop), being ready to re-direct them quickly with a high-value treat and keeping their bathroom area immaculate should be long-term strategies.

Now you know why we teach pottying on cue, how to choose a potty cue, how to reinforce it and why we do all this on leash. It's time to learn how to design a potty plan that works for your dog specifically.

CHAPTER 8

Your Dog's Personal Potty Plan

In this chapter, you'll learn how to predict when your dog will need the bathroom and how to design a tailored schedule that actually works for both of you.

Feeding for Success

Housetraining may be all about what happens at the back end of your dog, but figuring out when they need to go starts at the front end. Before you can create a schedule for your dog, you will need to take a closer look at what, when and how much you are feeding because all those things will dictate what, when and how much your dog will poop.

To be successful with housetraining, you have to make friends with the gastrocolic reflex because it's running the show. You can go back and review Chapter 2 if you're a keener, but all you really need to know is that what goes in must come out, and it will do so sooner rather than later. Remember, also, that even a small amount of food or a good long chew can trigger a potty event.

Housetraining That Works

It's worth repeating that if your dog is having normal stool quantity and volume, this is not the time to change their food. If, on the other hand, your dog has disproportionately large stools or is having an excessive number of bowel movements, then you may need to make some changes. Adult dogs will normally have two to five per day. Eight-to-ten-week-old puppies will normally have between five and eight poops a day. That might sound like a lot, but at that age, they are fed up to four times a day, and each meal will trigger a bowel movement. Add their wake-up poo and a before-bed poo and you're already up to six. Add a couple more after play or chew sessions and you can easily have eight per day. If your dog is producing more than the normal amount, there may be some irritation from their food.

By far the most common source of irritation is just feeding too much. Measure or weigh what you feed and keep your dog a little on the lean side. Learn to do a Canine Body Condition Score (see the Resources section at the back of this book), and make sure your dog sports a decent "tuck." If your dog is a little chunky *and* producing too many stools, reducing the amount you feed by 10%–30% will often resolve both problems. Don't bother telling me that you're only feeding what it says on the side of the bag. If your dog is overweight and pooping too much, either the amount the bag says to feed is wrong or what's in the bag is wrong for your dog.

Be especially careful about your feeding choices if you are dealing with one of the "fuel efficient breeds." Performance dog foods with higher protein and fat have their place, but unless your dog is working full-time, it's doubtful that you need them. Be very careful about potentially stressing their kidneys with elevated rates of protein or compromising their joints with excess weight.

Understanding where your dogs came from originally and what they would have eaten historically is essential. If you have a Labrador

Your Dog's Personal Potty Plan

Retriever, for instance, they were a fisherman's dog to begin with. Then duck hunting got added to their resume. Traditionally, they pretty much ate a little of whatever got caught or shot plus maybe some leftover oatmeal. They are economical to feed because their folks didn't have a lot to spare. They were designed to get fat on next to nothing—and they needed that fat because it kept them warm and buoyant when diving into freezing cold water to fetch ducks.

When you take that same Labrador and give them an urban lifestyle in a cozy apartment with no work beyond holding down a couch and the occasional walk, that tendency to put on fat easily no longer serves them well. Take the time to learn about your breed's purpose and traditional diet.

There is a lot of hype and pressure around feeding, and it often seems that the only thing two pet professionals can agree on is that the third one is doing it wrong! Part of your job as your dog's caregiver is to monitor their condition and make tailored choices for their optimum health. If what was recommended for your dog isn't working, then do some research and make an informed change.*

Keep an eye on the frequency, volume and colour of their urine, too. If they're peeing constantly, then it's probably time for a vet visit to eliminate the possibility of a bladder infection or something else going on. Another clue is the smell of the urine (colour is also informative but often hard to see). When excessive frequency is coupled with a really strong odour, my first inclination is to check the food. The most likely culprit is a "high-performance" food with a protein level that is surplus to your dog's needs. If the overly abundant

---

* See the Resources section at the back of the book for help with this.

pee is nearly odourless or colourless, then it's time to call the vet to make sure your pup is well enough to proceed with training.

Timing for Meals

Once you know your dog's general pattern, you can start tinkering with your timings. As a general rule, my dogs are not fed on a set schedule. Dogs who are fed at the same times every day may become anxious if their meal is delayed or when the clocks change. More importantly for me, dogs who expect breakfast at 7:00 AM on the dot are much more likely to pester me when I'm trying to have a cozy morning with coffee and a good book.

If your life never looks the same from one day to the next, please consider feeding your dog during a window of time rather than on a set schedule. A variation in feeding times of one or two hours is totally reasonable, especially if you're juggling the needs of children or elderly parents. You might also choose a "window of behaviour" —my own dogs know they will be fed in the morning sometime between barn chores and my own breakfast.*

If you have to leave the house at a particular time each day, then you'll need to pick a set feeding time that allows the gastrocolic reflex to kick in so you can get them empty before you dash off to conquer the world. It is still advisable that you train in some flexibility for their evening meal because it will help them stay calm if you're ever delayed getting home.

---

* With puppies or rescue dogs from traumatic backgrounds, begin with narrower windows. Fifteen to thirty minutes is a good starting point.

Your Dog's Personal Potty Plan

Setting Up a Potty and Supervision Schedule

If you're housetraining a young puppy, the schedule you start with is pretty much going to be dictated by them. You don't get much say in the early stages. All I can tell you is that it gets easier pretty quickly. If you don't cut too many corners in your training, the 5:00 AM (or earlier) potty runs will be a thing of the past in a matter of weeks.

If you're lucky enough to be housetraining a new-to-you adult dog or an older puppy, you might actually get to decide the times you're going to take them out based on what works for you instead of being at the relentless whim of puppy biology.

Even better, you might get a full night's sleep right from the start, but don't worry if the first couple are a bit wakeful. Just try to imagine what it would be like if one day someone moved you to a new home without advance notice. Now imagine that your former partner was gone and you had to adjust to a new one. A little compassion is in order here.

It's also worth mentioning that if you've been chosen by a dog with a tough history, they may be less than regular in their toilet habits because their access to food and water might have been less than regular too. They will need time to adjust.

It is highly advisable that you keep a housetraining log (pun intended, sorry), and you'll find a blank one in the Resources section at the back of this book. At the very least, put a sticky note on your exit door and keep a pen handy so you can write your dog's wake-up time and the time of your first potty run because that's your starting point for setting up a schedule.

Housetraining That Works

The next step is to figure out your dog's morning potty "style." Most dogs have a pattern for their first bathroom outing, and it is essential to know what it is. For instance, some dogs will go out for a quick pee but won't have a bowel movement until after breakfast. The occasional dog will have to poo before they can pee. Some dogs will pee, then poop, then pee again. If you take your dog out and they do both, but they have a poop accident five minutes after you go back in, you might have a "two-pooper." (If that happens at every outing, it's time to take another look at what they're eating or go see your veterinarian.)

Observe them carefully for the first three days and log all their excursions, successful or otherwise. Most dogs have an evening pattern, too. Although it's usually not as rigid, the information is still useful and needs to be included on your log.

My two dogs have very different patterns. In the morning, my Blue Lacy will either poop immediately or have a very quick pee and then have his bowel movement. He won't need to go again until long after breakfast. If we go for a walk, he's more than happy to pee on stuff in the woods but generally won't poop until we're nearly back at the car. In the evening, he is of the opinion that going out after 9:30 PM to do anything but pee is beneath him and believes that everyone should be in bed because he is. My Irish Setter, on the other hand, would prefer to dash out for the briefest of pees at about 6:30 AM and then come back in for snuggle time with my husband for at least another hour or more before she'll even consider going back out for a bowel movement. Her evening routine is more variable and depends on how busy her day was. If she did a lot of brain work or had a big field romp, she might conk out right after the post-dinner outing and be fine until morning. As she's still just a few months old, we usually insist on one last pee but if she appears to be glued to the couch, we don't push it.

Your Dog's Personal Potty Plan

Which of the following patterns best describes your dog's morning routine?

☐ Poop, then pee

☐ Pee, then poop

☐ Pee, poop, pee again

☐ Pee, poop, poop again, pee again ("two-poopers" often need to pee twice, too)

☐ Pee only, no poop until after breakfast

☐ My dog is a brilliant and creative artiste-de-potty with no discernible pattern

Now that you've established what needs to happen for the first outing of the day, you can start to build the rest of the routine.

Adult Dogs

Creating a schedule for an adult dog is pretty straightforward. After the first outing, bring them back inside and feed them breakfast. Keep them nearby and watch them carefully for any signs of restlessness. Take them out again anywhere from ten to thirty minutes after they've eaten. If they go, log it. If they don't, bring them in and either supervise closely* or return them to their confinement area. Log that, too. If you have multiple confinement

---

* "Supervise closely" is code for "don't even think about looking at a screen." If you're going to partake of pixels, please confine your dog. No exceptions.

options, choose the smallest one. For me, that means they'll be crated with something enticing to chew (to help trigger the gastrocolic reflex) or tethered to me while I write, read or putter around the house.

If they don't go, try again in half an hour. If you have three unsuccessful attempts half an hour apart, increase the intervals to one hour. Then two hours. If they're sleeping, don't wake them up to go out. Instead, just log the nap and take them out when they wake up of their own accord. When they finally go and you're sure they're empty, they can have a little free time in one area of the house as long as you're in it too. (This is not an option for dogs that leg-lift or mark until they've gone at least three weeks without incident.) Set a timer for twenty minutes and then go back to close supervision or confinement. After two weeks of no accidents, you can start increasing their free time by a minute or two each day.

Repeat after the evening meal and just before bed. For the pre-bedtime excursion, don't worry so much about a last poo unless they didn't have one after supper. Most adult dogs are able to manage overnight with just a late pee as long as no one is foolish enough to let them roam freely around the house all night. Confinement is not optional at this stage of training.

In between the morning and evening meals, the highest risk times for an accident are after a big play session, a prolonged chew, a walk or a pack status change (guests/dogs arriving or departing). Make sure to zip your dog outside for a chance to potty within a few minutes of these events. Over time, you will learn which of these is most likely to trigger your dog to need the bathroom and to what extent. Sometimes they'll just need to pee and other times they'll need to poo as well. If your dog tends to poop after all of these, anxiety may be playing a role. For future reference, the between-meal potty runs are also likely to be the first ones you'll be able to let your dog do solo.

The first few days of housetraining are seriously tedious. You'll do potty runs as frequently as new parents change diapers. Take heart—it gets easier in a hurry. After three to five days, you'll have a pretty good idea of when your dog actually has to go, and your dog will be getting the idea that you're out there for a reason. In five to seven days, your dog should be starting to pee on cue. In just a few more, you should be able to accurately predict when they'll need a bowel movement and get that happening on cue as well.

Puppies

Puppy schedules are also straightforward but a lot more labour intensive because they do everything more often. More meals, more naps, more play sessions, more treats, more chewing, more cell division, more behavioural stages. They are adorable and they are *relentless*.

Having a young puppy is as much work as a newborn human. Sure, they nap a lot, but they are also ambulatory, and our human brains often have trouble reconciling "tiny, helpless and vulnerable" with the reality of "self-propelled and able to wreak untold havoc in the blink of an eye."

It would be a disservice to tell you it gets easier in three to five days like it does with adult dogs. With puppies, it's more that the first three to five days can lure you into a false sense of competence. Enjoy it while you can because when they hit their stride and find out you are slow, functionally toothless, delicate-skinned, lacking protective fur, nose-blind and two legs short of the ideal, you'd better be ready.

Housetraining That Works

The good news is that you have thumbs and a pre-frontal cortex many times larger than theirs, and the "what did I get myself into" phase doesn't last very long. The first two weeks of housetraining and puppy-raising are the hardest. Need some good news? Puppies tend to learn their potty cues faster—mostly because they have less inhibition about going in front of people and because they go to the bathroom more often, so there are more opportunities to reward the correct behaviour.

While your housetraining journey begins the moment you bring your puppy home, the first steps in establishing a potty schedule are dictated by the moment your puppy wakes up (probably way earlier than you'd like). They will need to potty right away. The gap between when the eyes open and when the bladder lets go is minuscule. In the next chapter you'll learn how to do a potty run like a pro, but all you need to know right now is that whatever happens, write it on your log. What time was it? Did they pee? Did they poo? Did they seem nervous? Did they want to play, or were they eager to go back inside? Was it still dark out? Did they care? This is your starting point.

After that, you can build a schedule in much the same way as we do for adult dogs, with a couple notable adjustments. First, remember that they do everything more often. An adult dog might need to go outside after a meal or an afternoon nap, but a puppy needs to go out after *every meal and every nap*. Second, the amount of time between a triggering event and when they go is much shorter. Third, the amount of time they can be allowed freedom after they've emptied is about a tenth of what we'd allow an adult dog. So, set your timer for two minutes to start. Even better, just keep them close at hand with a house leash for the first couple weeks and then start allowing them three to five minutes of "semi-freedom." That is, just drop the leash rather than remove it.

Your Dog's Personal Potty Plan

If you log every excursion and every result, you will start to notice patterns. It might be that your pup needs to poo within five minutes of finishing their meal and that they have to pee immediately upon waking, but if they have a few slurps of water you are safe for a whole five minutes. Or maybe if you only play for a few minutes, they'll nap without having to go outside first. Your observations will help you know when you can take the time to put on shoes and when you need to *run*. As your puppy grows and the two of you start to work as a team, you'll be able to eliminate a meal or two and adjust your schedule as you lengthen the time between outings.

Important:

Puppy brains are lovely, malleable things. They learn quickly and retain most of what they learn and generally don't question things as much as would an adult dog with a history. It is easy to forget that they go through most of their major developmental stages before they're even a year old. We advanced primates are not programmed to change our parenting tactics that quickly and can often forget to raise the bar for our young dogs.

There are two stages that directly affect housetraining and are likely to catch an owner unaware. The first is the "flight instinct period." That's trainer jargon for "he used to be so good about just following me everywhere and then one day he just took off." Heartache and chaos are easily avoided by using a leash, house leash or dragline at all times until your puppy is nine to twelve months old. That way, you have a fair chance of actually getting hold of your dog when you know they need to go out. You have been warned.

The second is teething, which usually kicks in just as you're starting to pat yourself on the back for having trained a perfect puppy who never has accidents and always tells you when they need to go out. The

Housetraining That Works

first sign of teething isn't chewing—it's increased water consumption (because their mouth is on fire) and a tendency to wander into a room and just pee right in front of you as they distractedly stare into space. My theory is the pain in their mouth masks any minor sensations of fullness at the other end. Crates, x-pens and leashes will help. Provide plenty of safe chew items and consider freezing their water dish to cool their mouth and limit the amount they can drink at one time. This, too, shall pass.

CHAPTER 9

How to Do a Potty Run

Your personalized potty plan gives you a guideline for when your dog is likely to need the bathroom. Learning to predict *exactly* when they need to go and getting them there on time often requires more planning and skill than you might imagine.

Safety First

Your dog needs to be wearing a leash and collar for their potty runs. If you have a safely fenced yard, you can use pretty much anything that strikes your fancy, but if you have to potty your pup in a less secure space, you will need to be extra careful about your equipment choices.

The early days of housetraining with puppies are especially risky because they're still getting used to wearing a collar, and sometimes, they'll just suddenly put the brakes on and slip out backwards. It is beyond scary to find yourself suddenly holding a dangling, empty collar and see cars coming.

This behaviour is also common in adult dogs with negative associations to collars and leashes. If they were ever dragged towards something scary or unpleasant and found out they could escape

Housetraining That Works

by backing up and lowering their head, ducking out becomes an almost automatic response.

Check your collar to see how easily it pulls off. If your dog has a wide neck and a narrower head, it may be difficult to get the collar snug enough to stay put without having it be uncomfortably tight. In that case, my recommendation is that you get an all-cloth martingale collar. (See illustration.) These expand to fit over your dog's head but then tighten up just enough that dogs can't back out of them. When adjusted correctly, they tighten up just enough to prevent escapes and can be easily adjusted as your dog grows.

Martingale collar. These come in many variations. Some are wide, some are narrow. Some are made of a single material, some have a section of chain. All are based on the same basic design: one loop with two rings that goes around the dog's neck and a second loop with one ring (to attach a leash) that allows the collar to be tightened just enough to prevent escapes. This particular model also has a quick release buckle.

How to Do a Potty Run

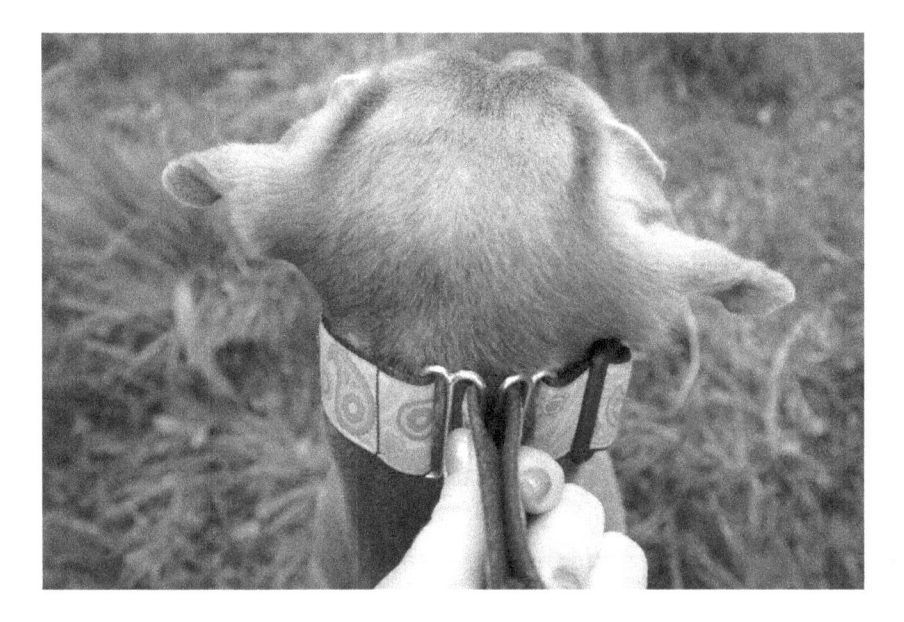

When a martingale is fitted correctly, the two rings should just meet when the collar is held at the base of the skull and pulled snug. Tally is modelling an extra wide martingale in a rather dapper paisley pattern.

Little Things That Make a Big Difference:

My dad always played with words, and one of his favourite re-written expressions was "Why suffer? Gladly learn from fools." While quite capable of heeding that advice in most areas of my life, when it comes to dogs, I have been a fool many times over. Every tip in this section was learned the hard way. Save yourself the pain and learn it the Papa way.

(If your dog wears a harness, please be aware that many of those also slip off easily.)

Housetraining That Works

The day you bring a new dog home, do not take them in the house until they've at least peed outside in the spot you want them to go. Drive around for another hour or two if you have to. Carry them around until your arm is cramping. Feed them. Play with them. Give them water. Just *do not let them set foot on the floor of their new home until they've gone to the bathroom at least once where you want them to go*. The first place they go in a new place is likely to be their default when you slip up on supervision or timing, so make sure that default is the place you actually want them to use.

When your dog wakes you up in the morning and needs to go pee, chances are good that you do too. If you experience any degree of bladder urgency, I recommend you go first. Yes, that increases the chance of an accident in their crate or pen, but that really isn't the end of the world. If you live anywhere with a degree of privacy, you may opt for getting the puppy out first. If it takes a little longer than expected for puppy to get busy and your needs are somewhat more pressing than anticipated, you wouldn't be the first person to, ahem, "model the correct behaviour" for your dog. Not talking about myself, obviously.

It's already hard enough to get a puppy out fast enough to prevent accidents. This is not the time to be fiddling with a teeny, tiny collar with a teeny, tiny buckle and trying to attach a teeny, tiny leash while holding a teeny, tiny wiggly puppy. Or a giant wiggly puppy. Or a seriously happy newly adopted dog that is just starting to realize that this going outside thing happens every day now. Do yourself a favour and attach the leash to the collar before you slip it over your pup's head. Get in the habit of leaving the collar and leash on top of your dog's crate at night (or hanging up by the exit door with your keys and headlamp).

Sleep in pyjamas for the first couple weeks, even if you don't usually, or keep a bathrobe handy. Make sure it has good pockets.

How to Do a Potty Run

If you choose a bathrobe, tie the belt in a knot rather than a bow because the likelihood of your puppy untying it is directly correlated to whether you're wearing underwear and your neighbours are watching.

If you're going out in the middle of winter, make sure that you have a warm coat to wear. Leave it by the door with bags and treats pre-loaded in the pockets.

Whatever the weather, your boots or shoes should be the kind that just slip on because you're not going to have time for anything else those first few runs.

Have your keys on a lanyard and hanging up where you can grab them as you race for the door. Make sure you put that lanyard around your neck rather than dangling out of your pocket. It is far too easy to dislodge them when adding treats and poo bags, and the only thing worse than being stuck outside with a puppy in freezing cold weather, waiting for them to pee, is discovering you've locked yourself out. Not telling you how I know that. Oh, and while we're on the subject, make sure that lanyard is tucked inside your shirt when you bend over to bag a poop lest the learning curve claim another victim. Cleaning poo off a key is almost as much fun as not noticing the yuck factor until after you've stuck it in the lock or back in your pocket.

If it will be dark when you go out, having a headlamp is a really good idea. You've got to have one hand free to hold the leash and another to give a treat and then scoop poop. You will not have another to spare for holding a cell phone or a flashlight. If you drop a flashlight, it will land on the ground. If you drop your phone, it will land in the poop. Thanks, Murphy.

Housetraining That Works

Are You Ready?

Almost. You have all of your equipment ready to go, there's a potty log near the door and you've cleverly learned how not to lock yourself out or freeze to death thanks to my virtuoso-level mistake-making. You even know some general guidelines for when your dog will need to potty, but can you tell just by looking at them that it's go-time?

Housetraining gets a lot easier when you can recognize "pee face." If you carefully observe your dog during their high-risk windows, you will start to notice a particular facial expression that precedes both successful runs and inconvenient puddles. They may appear vaguely distracted. They might look at you but seem oddly unfocused. Or they'll stare into space and look as if they hear the sound of moths breeding in South America. Remember that look because as far as I can tell, they're listening to their own bladder getting ready to explode.

You're also going to spend more time looking at your dog's butt than anyone ever warned you about. Learn to spot the difference between an innie, an outie and a "turtle head." When your dog is empty, the area around the anus should actually be a little concave.* When it flattens out to a neutral position, you need to think about getting them outside soon. If it's starting to bulge, that puppy really needs to go poo right now.

Occasionally, you may be watching your puppy and suddenly realize that their bum is dilating, and the puppy hasn't even stopped playing because they're so engaged with what they're doing that they don't

---

* In older dogs, especially older males, that area can stick out a little more, and it may take a few days for you to recognize what "empty" looks like.

How to Do a Potty Run

even realize they need to poop. Don't hesitate—just scoop them up and get outside. (Bet you're glad they're already wearing their leash and collar.)

If your dog has a fuzzy butt, seriously consider trimming enough of the hair that you can see their anus clearly. Don't attempt this when they're extra wiggly, and use blunt-ended scissors for safety. Even better, make an appointment with a groomer for an initial get-acquainted session and ask them to tidy it up a bit.

Another good reason to feed your dog carefully and keep their hind end "landscaped" is because upset tummies and hairy bottoms are a bad combo. That's a full bath situation, and bathing a dog with a pasty butt is just plain nasty. My best advice if this happens to you? Wear gloves and, above all, keep your mouth closed until they're fully clean. You can probably guess how I learned that.

The Potty Run (at last!)

We'll start with the first run of the day and gear it to the needs of a very young puppy. You can tailor the run for adult dogs with just a few minor changes.

For the first three to five days with a new puppy, when it's time to go out, just scoop them up, being sure to support their hind end, and slip the collar (with pre-attached leash because you're a housetraining rockstar) over their head (you could say "noses" if you're awake enough to make words—more on that later) as you race for the door. Hook the index finger of your dog-carrying hand through the collar, from front to back, to prevent puppy from wiggling free and discovering that gravity is not their friend. If you need a hand free for doors or elevator buttons, throw the handle end of the leash

Housetraining That Works

over one shoulder so it doesn't trip you or get caught in the elevator door. Slip on your shoes and put your key lanyard around your neck. As, you open the door, you might say, "Out we go!" in the cheeriest tone you can muster at 4 AM.

If you have stairs, carry your pup down them for as long as you can manage—their joints are mostly soft cartilage at this age and must be protected. If your pup has only just been introduced to the collar and leash, please carry them all the way to their potty spot before putting them on the ground. Now is not the time for a leash lesson. Over the next few days, you can gradually carry them less distance because once they understand the point of the exercise they will likely race for their potty spot as soon as their paws hit the ground.

If you have an elevator ride in between you and the potty area, *do not put your puppy down until you are safely outside*. Or carry a full clean-up kit. Your choice.

Once you arrive at the potty area, you need to switch gears from "Battle stations, people—Go, go, go!" to doing your best impression of a tree. Be as quiet and boring as possible while also intermittently engaging in the interpretive dance necessary to avoid being hog-tied by the decidedly non-linear being at the other end of the leash.

There are a limited number of outcomes for the first potty run of the day:

1. Puppy will go to the bathroom. (Reward them and celebrate with play and exploration.)
2. Puppy will want to play or explore or both. (Don't. Because you're a tree.)

How to Do a Potty Run

3. Puppy will park their cute little butt and act like you're the one that woke *them*.
4. Puppy will act like their only mission in life is to get back inside.

If you were successful on the first try, record the details on your potty log and make sure to take pictures (of your puppy, not the poop) and call all your friends to tell them how smart your dog is. Cross-post on every possible social media platform, and feel free to tag me @zoemacbean so I can admire your clever pup, too. This is the first big success of your dog-training journey, and you should probably mark the occasion with a new pair of shoes at the very least. I'm only exaggerating a little. Seriously, this is momentous and worthy of celebration.

If your puppy shows no inclination to get down to business, you are not obligated to stay out there forever waiting for them to go. Three to five minutes is plenty. If they don't go, pick them up and head back inside. Record the non-event and set a timer for fifteen to thirty minutes to remind you to repeat the process. Feed your pup their breakfast to help trigger the gastrocolic reflex, but supervise closely and be ready to dash outside again. If there's still nothing happening, carry the puppy around while you make coffee one-handed until it's time to try again. Repeat until pup is successful. Remind yourself why you got a dog. It will get easier.

All the other potty runs of the day are just repeats of the first one but a little easier because you're already awake and dressed and, unless you've put them in their crate or x-pen for a nap, your puppy is already wearing their collar and leash.

> **Pro Tip:**
>
> If your pup seems overwhelmed or reluctant and is frozen in place, it may help to create a little "potty trail" of small high-value treats placed two or three inches apart in a circle or spiral starting at your dog's nose. Once they begin sniffing, snacking and circling, they will often relax enough to go. Reward and celebrate (but perhaps a little quieter than you would with a bolder pup).

Adult Dogs

There are a few important differences between puppy and adult potty runs. The biggest is that you usually get a full night's sleep before the first run of the day. After the first three to five days, adult dogs will get taken outside less often because you'll have a pretty good idea of their pattern by then. They can also usually make it outside on time without being carried. If they are empty, they might be able to handle twenty minutes of freedom before they go back to supervision and confinement protocols, and if they don't go when you take them out, you can probably wait a little longer before trying again. The only real downside is that adult dogs take a little longer to learn their potty cues because they just don't go as often.

Next Steps

All you have to do now is remember to reward successes and keep track of when your puppy actually went, what exactly they did and whether it happened in the right place or was an accident. (We'll be talking more about how to handle accidents in Chapter 12.) If you log everything for

How to Do a Potty Run

the first two weeks (four weeks for adult dogs), you'll get to know your pup well enough to accurately predict when they need to go out and when they can be allowed a little more freedom in the house.

After that, you really don't have to worry about keeping a log again unless they go through a phase of having accidents again. Don't panic if that happens—just go back to logging until you can figure out the pattern. In puppies, suddenly peeing in the house after several weeks of no accidents usually signals the onset of teething. Other common culprits for a broken success streak can be clock changes, medical issues, not adjusting your timings as puppy grows* and good old handler errors. *Track it to trace it.*

Sneaky Trainer Bonus Behaviour #2: Noses

After three to five days of just putting the collar (with attached leash, of course) over your dog's head, and maybe even saying "Noses!" it's time to teach them to volunteer for the job. If your dog's crate door opens from left to right, use your right hand to pick up the collar-and-leash combo and slide it onto your left arm, letting it hang about halfway between your wrist and elbow. Pick up a treat with your left hand. Using your right hand, open the crate door just enough that you can reach in with your left hand and offer your dog the treat. As they take the treat, use your right hand to slide the collar over their head as you say "Noses!" After a couple days of this, you can just hold the collar in your right hand and hold your left hand with the treat just inside it.

---

* Oddly, sometimes your dog's increasing ability to hold it for longer can undermine your success. For instance, if you're still taking them out immediately after play sessions but they now can hold it for ten minutes longer, you might be back inside and thinking they didn't really need to go only to have them pee inside five minutes later.

Housetraining That Works

This is how we get ready for the "Noses" exercise. Note the treat in the left hand, the pre-attached leash and the right hand holding the martingale open.

If you're very dexterous, you can use your treat-holding hand to open the latch. I usually let go of the collar, open the latch and pick up the collar again.

How to Do a Potty Run

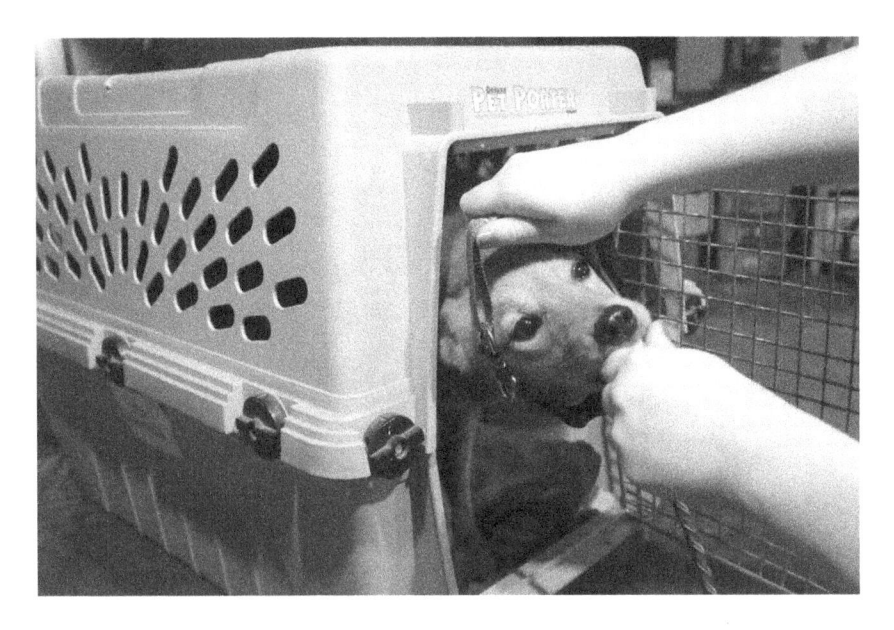

As Kova reaches for the treat, her person pulls back the treat-holding hand to lure their dog into the collar.

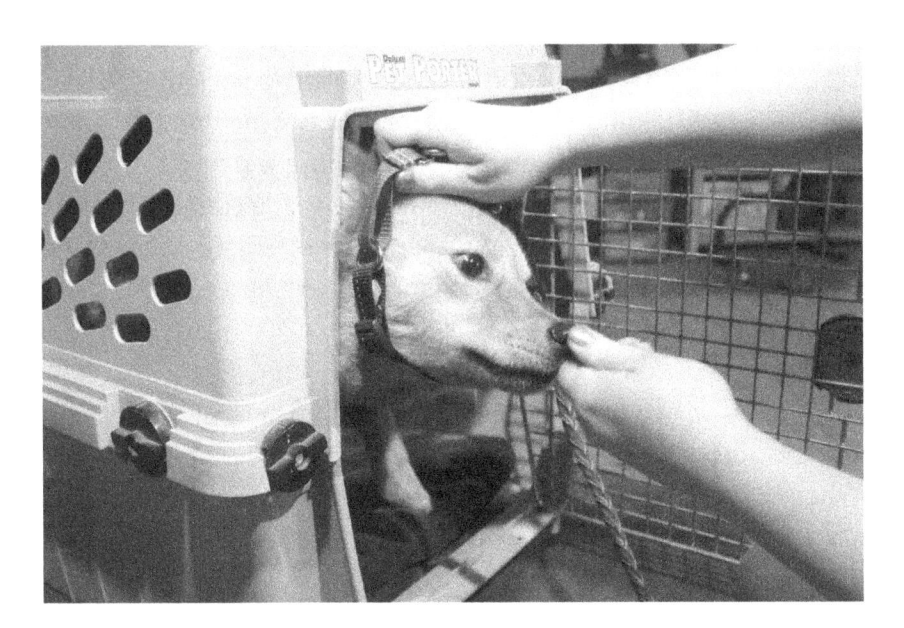

Halfway there. Keeping the treat close to your dog's face will encourage them to push forward into the collar.

Housetraining That Works

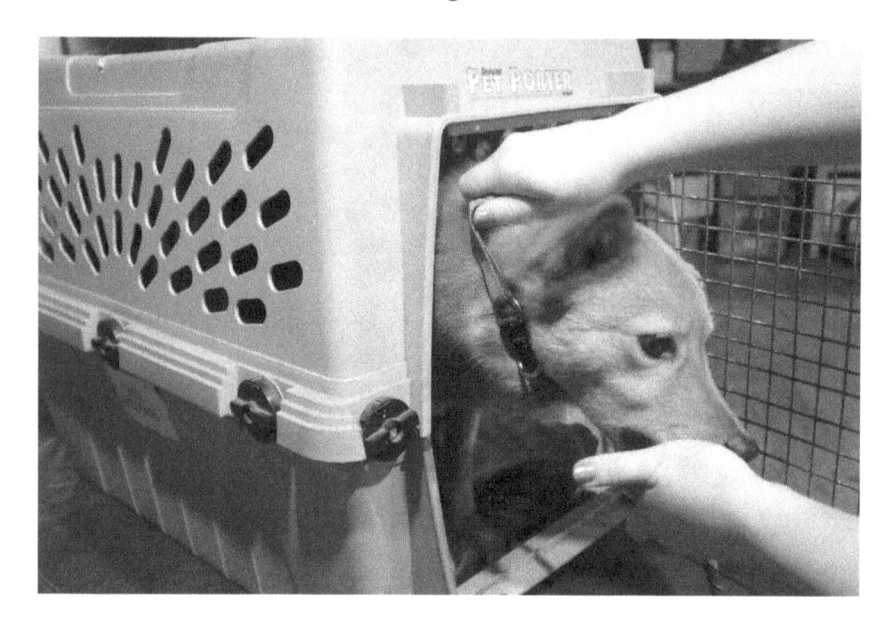

Success! This technique is especially helpful for wiggly puppies, but works well on older dogs too.

When you start to see your dog leaning forward to get into the collar, you can start holding the treat an inch or two behind the collar. Don't say, "Noses!" until you're sure that nose is going to make it all the way through. The reason we could say the cue word before this was that we were the ones in charge of getting the collar all the way on, and we could consistently predict the outcome. Now the dog gets to choose.

After a day or two of that, you can probably just hold the collar in front of their face and wait for them to poke their head through. When they do, make sure you suddenly remember there's a treat in your pocket just for super clever and helpful dogs who get dressed all by themselves.

There will come a morning when your dog decides that outdoors is more exciting than doing the stupid collar thing and they'll try to

How to Do a Potty Run

dodge it. Just close the crate door and wait a few seconds before opening it again and presenting their collar. It may take a few tries, but they'll soon dive into their collar whenever it's presented.

Make sure to continue rewarding them until they make it clear that they like doing this and they've made the connection between putting on their collar and going outside. After that, going outside is probably sufficient reinforcement for the behaviour. While this isn't really an essential skill, it's still seriously handy (you'll thank me if you ever put your back out), easy to teach and very brag worthy.

CHAPTER 10

Building Control

Take a moment to pat yourself on the back. You have come so far, and the hardest part is over. If you've done your homework and haven't cut too many corners, your dog is now able to go to the bathroom on cue and on leash. They should also have a fairly regular bathroom pattern by now, and you may have gained something of a reputation as a "potty psychic" for your ability to accurately predict whether any dog within your sight needs to poop or pee.

When you've gone three weeks without accidents, or with maybe only one or two puddles by the exit doors, your dog is functionally housetrained. At least, they are housetrained to the best of their current physical ability and your observation skills. All that's left to do now is to develop their bladder and bowel control and teach them to signal their needs clearly.

If you have a puppy, please understand that any significant level of control doesn't really happen until they are at least five months old and usually more like nine months. Or more. Generally speaking, the larger your breed, the longer they will take to mature. Just like with children, every dog is an individual and will develop in their own time.

If you're training an adult dog, keep in mind that if they've been out in a back yard or kept in a run their whole life, they may have little or no control because there was never a reason to develop any.

Housetraining That Works

Building control takes time, and the fastest way forward is a two-pronged approach. First, make sure you're not accidentally sabotaging your dog's progress. Second, intentionally create multiple situations where your dog will have to do "mini holds."

What Not to Do

After the first three to five "get acquainted" days with a new puppy or adult dog, politely ignore any helpful suggestions that you should take your dog out every half hour or every hour. That's a really great way to teach them to never bother holding it.

Same goes for just letting them hang out in the back yard, going wherever and whenever they want. The first few weeks with a new dog can be pretty intense. Even more so with a puppy. It can be very tempting to cut a few corners just so you can breathe or maybe even eat. There will come a day when you can just let them out while you take a moment for yourself, but now is not the time. To avoid complications further down the road, your best practice right now is to "make haste slowly."

Dog doors and doors left open in nice weather are also problematic because a dog door might not always be available or advisable,* and nice weather has a habit of changing.

---

* Where I live, a dog door is an open invitation for critters to walk in your house and trash the place. It is not easy to convince a dog that they are not allowed to pee in the house after a bear has done so. Don't think your local beasties could fit through yours? Don't worry, they're always happy to enlarge it for you.

Building Control

Small Things That Make a Huge Difference

One really cool side benefit of intentionally teaching control is that just about anything you do to make them wait a little will actually make your dog an even more charming companion. Have you ever noticed that kids with rather formal manners are extra adorable? Same goes for dogs.

The first and easiest way to develop control is to adjust the way you feed them. If you feed your dog out of a bowl, they'll probably wolf it down in about ten seconds flat. When they finish eating, young puppies will need to go to the bathroom anywhere from right now to two minutes later. Adult dogs might give you five to thirty minutes.

Consider dividing their food into two separate experiences. Part one can be hand-fed to them on a "learn to earn" basis while you teach them a few simple behaviours.

What you teach is entirely up to you, but there is one behaviour that you'll want to avoid. While "Sit" is generally the first thing that almost every other puppy training book says you should teach, it really isn't very helpful in the early stages of housetraining. If your dog really needs the bathroom, squatting to sit can easily lead to system overload.

My own dogs learn a folding style "Down" as their first formal position. Think of the way a Border Collie drops—either the front end goes down first or both ends go down together. No "danger zone" squatting on the way.

The other half of your dog's meal can be loaded into an interactive feeder—like a puzzle ball or snuffle mat. They'll still need to go out when they finish, but it will take longer to finish eating. Their gastrocolic reflex will still get triggered, but your dog will want to finish eating, so they'll tend to hold it a little longer without even realizing. So easy and surprisingly effective.

Next, we start building behaviours that create micro-delays around exits and build some useful rituals around feeding too.

Sneaky Trainer Bonus Behaviour #3: Wait Politely for Meals

One of my favourite behaviours for building control also builds self-control and frustration tolerance. I've always called it "Puppy Zen"* because in order to get the treat, they must not try to get the treat. It's easy to teach and will serve you well throughout your dog's life.

---

* Thirty or forty years ago, I used to teach this as "Leave it!" but, no matter how many times they were reminded, my students could not seem to stay quiet and wait for the correct behaviour. My classes echoed with "leave it, leave it, leave it!" —while their puppies all dove for the treats.

Credit goes to Karen Pryor, founder of clicker training and one of my favourite humans of all time, for being the first to show me how to model silence and capture behaviours as they naturally occurred. I renamed it "Puppy Zen" to evoke a sort of monastic stillness and removed any command language from my homework sheets. Voilà! Quiet classes and self-restraining dogs.

I would be seriously remiss if I did not also mention Susan Garrett's It's Yer Choice (IYC) game.

While most innovative trainers incorporate some level of indirect access training in their programs, Susan takes the basic skill of waiting politely for food or toys and turns it into the foundation for truly brilliant, advanced work. Her visionary, science-based approach has revolutionized both competitive agility and pet dog training. She's nothing short of a Canadian national treasure.

Building Control

Start by placing one piece of their dinner in your closed palm. Keep the rest of their meal in your pocket or in a small bowl nearby but out of reach. Allow your puppy to sniff and lick your hand but keep your hand closed. If you are training a very rambunctious dog and there are way too many teeth and toenails coming in contact with your skin, you may want to use your house leash to tether your dog to a doorknob and sit just out of reach.

At some point, your dog will either stop licking and sniffing or they will pull away ever so slightly. Whether they're on the verge of giving up or planning their next assault, as soon as they pull away, quickly say, "Yes!" open your hand, say, "Get it!" and let them have it.

After a couple successful repetitions, start making them wait until you pick up the treat with your other hand and give it to them. Remember to say "Get it" each time. If they dive in before you give permission, just close your hand and wait. Say nothing and be still. Let them figure this out on their own.

Gradually work up to having them offer more elaborate behaviours— maybe backing up two or three steps, making eye contact or offering a down. Name those behaviours as they appear. You may even be able to hold the treat in your open palm for several seconds and have your pup wait politely for permission.

At this point you can start using your dog's stuffed interactive feeder just like a treat. Hold it in your hands and wait for your dog to back up or do any behaviour that shows self-restraint. Say, "Yes!" and "Get it!" as you place the feeder on the ground.

Over time, you can grow this behaviour to include any food or any toy until your dog can easily hang out at a picnic or around children playing without you having to worry about stolen food or toys snatched out of small hands.

Notice the absence of a "command" or cue for this behaviour. That is a deliberate choice. The cue in this case is the stillness of my hand or my whole body. You shouldn't have to tell your dog not to grab things out of your hand. That should be the default. You only need a cue to tell them when they may do so.

Sneaky Trainer Bonus Behaviour #4: Stillness

After the first twenty-four to forty-eight hours with your pup, start waiting for a tiny moment of stillness before you open their crate or x-pen to let them out. Just pause with your hand on the latch or near it. Look a little bit past them rather than making eye contact. Wait until they stop throwing themselves at the door or jumping up. It might only be a split-second but if you mark the moment with "Yes!" and open the door promptly they will quickly figure it out.

Over the next few days, grow the behaviour by waiting for a longer pause or even for them to back up a little. Make them give you a second little pause if they start to go bananas when you reach to unlatch the door. Just freeze and wait them out.

Sneaky Trainer Bonus Behaviour #5: Release Word

Once your dog is recognizing your stillness as a sign that they, too, should be still, you are ready to teach a release word. You can easily introduce it in combination with the last behaviour—just start saying, "Break!" when you open the door.

Building Control

After a couple repetitions, start to open the door in slow motion. If your dog tries to charge out, just pause and close the door gently. Wait until they're still again and open the door about one inch. If they stay still, say "Break!" and open the door. The first time might take several repetitions, so maybe don't introduce this on the first run of the day if your pup still has trouble making it outside on time. Grow the behaviour until you can open the door all the way and count to three before releasing your dog.

Sneaky Trainer Bonus Behaviour #6: Luring

This is a deceptively simple behaviour that is so frequently used by trainers that we often take it for granted and forget that not everyone knows how to teach it to their dogs. It's a really good choice when building bladder and bowel control because it keeps your puppy moving and engaged with you without them having to learn something complicated. Perfect for when they're teething and temporarily misplace their brains.

To teach luring, just put a treat between your thumb and second finger. Keep your index finger extended. Touch the treat to your puppy's nose and move it forward slowly while you make a little kiss-kiss sound. Encourage them to follow it and when they've taken a step or two forward, say "Yes" and "Get it" and let them have the treat.

The reason we touch the treat to their nose and make kissy sounds is because that's what tells them it's okay to try to get the treat. If you've done your homework and played Puppy Zen, your dog might be reluctant to follow your hand, so you will need to add these "discriminative stimuli" so they can understand when it's okay to follow a lure and when they need to keep their butts parked.

Housetraining That Works

Treat touched to nose + kiss-kiss sounds = okay to follow. Treat not touched to nose + permission not given = do not try to get treat.

When they can lure several steps, change hands, and maybe go the other direction. Now see if you can lure in a circle or a wiggly line. Now try luring their nose to the ground or sit on the ground and lure them under and over your legs. (If they're too big for this, try grabbing a door frame and luring them under your arm.)

A dog following a cookie may not seem like a big deal, but what happens next will make a huge difference in your training relationship. Once your dog will lure with either hand, in just about any direction, it's time to transition from bribe to paycheque.

Go back to the very first step, but this time, leave the treat in the non-luring hand. Touch your index finger to their nose, make the kiss-kiss noise and lure forward just a step or two. If they follow, say "Yes" and quickly reward with the treat from the other hand. Remember to say, "Get it."

If they don't follow and give you a look that suggests you've lost it, show them the treat in the non-lure hand, then close that hand again and repeat the touching of the index finger to the nose and moving forward a little. If they even just stretch their nose out a bit, mark that with a "yes" and reward quickly from the other hand.

If you keep showing them the treat in the non-lure hand and then playing dumb as if you have no idea what the problem is, the vast majority of dogs will decide to follow the finger in hopes that you'll get the hint and remember how to dispense treats. Make sure you do.

If, after several tries, your dog has clearly given up on you, try putting the treat in the luring hand but only touching your finger to their nose. When they follow, say "Yes—get it!" and toss the treat out in the direction you were luring. After a few of those, try one with the treat back in the non-luring hand.

You may have to mix it up a bit at first—switching back and forth between no treat in hand or empty hand, especially when introducing a new behaviour. Soon your dog will go just about anywhere you want simply by touching their nose and moving your hand. (You can drop the kiss-kiss noise if you like). Your dog will learn to relax and focus on what you're trying to teach because they know you can be trusted to pay up.

Sneaky Trainer Bonus Behaviour #7: Step Up (Stationing)

Another brag-worthy behaviour is teaching dogs to "station"— that is to put themselves on an elevated platform when asked and stay put. For now, we'll be asking them to put just their front feet on a smaller object such as a step stool or an upside down rubber feed pan. It's a fairly simple skill to teach and is ridiculously useful both in its own right and as a foundation for all manner of future behaviours.

Choose your "station" carefully. It should be non-skid, non-tippy, portable and quiet when moved or stepped on. For healthy adult dogs, it cannot be any higher than their elbows. Half that for puppies or older dogs with orthopaedic issues.

It could be as simple as piece of wood, a single level step stool or a piece of high-density foam. My favourite is rubber feed pans because they're affordable, stable, portable and, above all, *versatile*. At our house there are several expensive purpose-made dog platforms and they're pretty fabulous but none of them doubles as a toy that can be flung to reward a dog after a particularly brilliant bit of work. My dogs love their "farmyard frisbees."

To teach this behaviour, place your stationing target on the floor between you and your dog. Touch a treat to their nose and lure them over it. Some dogs will immediately put their feet on it. When they do, say "Yes" and reward them. Get in the habit of using your release word to let them off because that's the foundation for teaching Stays later on.

Less confident dogs may be quite determined to avoid touching it. They may hop over it, bump it, walk around it or just generally try to deny its existence. You will need to sharpen your training skills a bit and look for tiny little successive approximations of what you want. Maybe their foot hovered over it for a nano-second or they bumped it when backing up to avoid it. Mark and reward each of these little behaviours and be patient while your dog develops a better picture of what you're looking for.

In two or three sessions, your dog will be able to confidently place their front feet on the target object. Now you can start moving the target to different locations and placing it a little further away from you. See if you can get your dog to step on it by just looking at them and then pointedly looking at the target. You might also want to introduce a cue for the behaviour to make it easier to introduce other objects. We use "Step up."

Why are we teaching this? Well, in the long run, it will be tremendously useful to station your dog to pose for pictures, do conditioning exercises or just wait politely for guests to enter.

Learning how to teach it will also significantly advance your training skills.

Building Control

For right now, though, the most important thing is that when their front feet are elevated, they are a lot less likely to squat and pee. Having your dog station makes it so much easier for them to wait at the door while you put on your shoes or fiddle with keys.

If you have a large breed puppy and a long elevator ride between your apartment and the potty area, take your feed pan with you and ask your dog to "step up" for the duration of the ride. You may have to reinforce with treats a couple extra times but it sure beats trying to clean up an accident one-handed while the other passengers glare at you.

Sneaky Trainer Bonus Behaviour #8: Ready? (Eye Contact)

Another thing you can do to create a bladder-building delay at the exit door is to teach them to make eye contact before they go out. For the first three days with a puppy, just open the door and say, "Out you go!" as you run for the potty area. After three days, put your hand on the doorknob and just wait for a second or two for that puppy to look up at you. The minute they flick their eyes up at you, even if it's just to see why the service is so lousy, say "Out you go" and open the door. Once they're clear that looking at you gets them access to outside, you can start adding a cue as their head tilts up. We use "Ready?"

Sneaky Trainer Bonus Behaviour #9: Back Up

Some puppies won't flick their eyes up to you—they'll actually just back up a step or two. The minute you see them back up, mark the behaviour with a "Yes!" and open the door as you say, "Out you go." Build the behaviour to the point where your dog will back up several steps so they're completely clear of the door. Now add a cue. My verbal cue for backing up is "Beep, beep" when we're practicing tricks but at doorways my dogs know to look for my expectantly raised eyebrows as a cue for them to remember their manners.

Sneaky Trainer Bonus Behaviour #10: Wait

Now that your pup knows they have to back up a bit or look at you (or maybe even both) before you'll open the door and let them out, it's time to teach them that even if the door is open they must wait for permission.

All you have to do to grow this behaviour is cue eye contact or backing up and then jiggle the doorknob. If your dog moves forward, just freeze and wait for them to back up or look at you again. When they do, praise them and say, "Out you go" and open the door.

When they can ignore a doorknob jiggle, try cracking the door an inch. If they push forward, close the door, wait and try again. Now try two or three inches. Then halfway open. Pretty soon, your dog will wait even if the door is all the way open. Car doors should have the same rules.

Beyond good manners, this behaviour is a safety feature and may someday save your dog's life. You only once have to open your front door to find three bear cubs on the porch (and their mama right behind them) to realize how important this is. Same goes for mail carriers, parcel delivery people, elderly relatives or your neighbour's fundraising children coming up your walkway.

You may introduce a cue but you can also just decide that the default is waiting. You may have noticed that I don't use their usual release

Building Control

word (Break!) here. That's because, in the context of housetraining, "Out you go" functions as a release word but also as a sort of pre-cue for the potty run.

As a bonus, while they're waiting, they are also developing control. Watch them closely, especially very young puppies. If you see them start to circle or squat, just pick them up and *run*. "Wait" can wait.

Sleepy Trainer Bonus Behaviour: Sleeping In

Just because your eight-week old puppy woke you up at 5 AM doesn't mean your eight-month old gets to do that. After your first couple weeks, you may notice that your dog has decided to be merciful and let you sleep a whole fifteen minutes extra. At that point, you can start adding five or ten minutes of horizontal bliss to your alarm time every few days until it's where you want it to be.

Your pup may fuss but by now you should be able to tell the difference between the sounds that mean disaster is imminent and the ones that just mean they'd rather you got up and played with them. Wait for a couple seconds of quiet before you take them out.

Remember that your dog needs at least 14-16 hours of sleep every day. To make sure you both get a good night's sleep, consider limiting their water for an hour before lights out and do one last potty run before you go to bed.

CHAPTER 11

Learning a Signal

It's time to let you in on a little secret: this step is optional. Yes, having a dog who will tell you they need to go out is useful, but it isn't, strictly speaking, essential. There are plenty of well-housetrained dogs who don't know how to intentionally signal their owners. As long as *you* know when they need to go, you don't actually have to teach your dog to signal you. Let's review your options so you can make an informed choice.

Watch for Potty Face

Your first and easiest option is closely observing your dog for telltale signs they need to go out. Parents who ask their child if they need to pee before putting on a snowsuit or beginning a long car ride already know the answer to the question. Yes. Yes, they do. No matter what the kid says.

In much the same way, if your dog seems unable to settle or to concentrate and you're about to start cooking or watching a movie, ask them if they need to go out. (Pacing, circling, farting and staring into space with a faintly furrowed brow are also good tells.) Whatever their response, trust your instincts and take them out. If they go, celebrate your brilliant observation skills and be sure to compliment your dog on their extreme cleverness. If they don't, keep a very close eye on them when you go back in. Ideally, use one of your confinement strategies—especially if what you have to do next involves a screen or paying attention to children. Try again later.

Learn Their Potty Language

Your second choice is to notice if your dog has made any subtle attempts to communicate their needs to you and reinforce one of those until it's actually noticeable. If, for example, your dog's only sign that they need to go is them staring at the door and willing it to open, you're not going to notice that from the next room. To grow this behaviour into something useful, you might have to do your best "What is it, girl? Is Timmy trapped down the well?" routine until your dog either whines, grunts or wiggles in frustration. You can respond by suddenly remembering how the door opens and taking them outside.

One of my favourite dogs was far too much of a gentleman to draw attention to his own needs. If he needed the bathroom he would quietly go to the door, put his back to it, sit with his hind legs crossed and stare at me intently—through the wall. If anyone happened to walk by and ask if he needed out, he would sort of shiver as if it was all he could do to hold it in. Clearly, there would be no barking to be let out with this fellow. Eventually he learned to bump the door with his head, shoulder and backside when he turned and sat down but he never quite got over looking apologetic for having summoned us. Thump, thump, thump—still miss you, Harley.

These days, the go-to signal for my weird little blue dog is a sort of tippy-tappy dance, and it works very well for him. If he starts to tap dance in the middle of the night, the clickety sound of his toenails will wake me up. He also has a funny little low grunting sound that means things are rather urgent. If we ask if he needs out and he

Learning a Signal

makes a sharp chirping sound, he has an upset tummy, and we better move fast. We didn't need to teach him any of these signals. Careful observation revealed them, and everyone in the house reinforced them.

Not all dogs are reticent about getting your attention, and it's worth taking a moment to choose a signal that you can live with. Some people don't mind a dog barking to be let out. Trainers generally find "bossy barking" highly undesirable. (Translation: it's obnoxious and we hate it.) Same goes for scratching at the door. Less likely to bother your neighbours but still irritating.

If your dog tends to express their needs with behaviour you find objectionable, you will have to spend some time watching for the quieter behaviours that happen just before the unwanted ones and reinforce those like crazy.

Teach a Signal

Third on the list is teaching your dog a completely new signal. The most common is ringing a bell*. The technique is fairly simple—hang a couple bells on a ribbon from the door handle of your dog's potty exit door at nose level. Smear a little something yummy on the ribbon and encourage your dog to investigate it. When they lick the yummy thing, the bells will ring, and you can open the door and take them out.

After a couple days, you can start to ask if they need to go out just as they reach out their nose to nudge the ribbon. In a couple

---

* Pre-recorded speech buttons are another option. If your dog showed a lot of talent for stationing, these could be a really fun choice.

more days you can stop putting yummy stuff on the ribbon but instead reward them by hand. Soon your dog will ring the bell on their own if they want out. Ta-dah! Your friends will be terribly impressed, and you will never have another housetraining accident, right? Well…

Yes, your friends will be impressed, but there are some potential pitfalls that rarely get mentioned. Your dog might be scared of the bells. That can usually be worked through, but maybe now is not the best time—dogs need to be relaxed and confident to be successful at on-leash pottying. Or your dog might associate the bells a little too closely with going out, so if you ring them by accident when you answer the door, you might trigger a potty incident (just for your dog, not your guests!).

By far the most common issue with bells is the problem of the fake ring. At some point in the training process, your dog will figure out they can make you open the door anytime they like. They'll ring that bell a dozen extra times a day because they want to go outside and generate some pee so that you'll give them a cookie. Or because it got attention. Or because the neighbour's cat is being weird again and they must investigate. Then, the one time you don't take them out, there's a puddle by the door.

If you are an experienced dog owner and can read your dog well, the problem isn't hard to fix as long as you're still taking your dog out on leash. If it's clear after a couple minutes outside that the bell ringing was a false alarm, just go back inside without doing anything fun and return to close supervision. A few days of that usually makes it clear that the bells are for potty events only.

If this is your first dog, I would gently suggest that ringing bells or pushing buttons to be let out could wait a few months and that

Learning a Signal

you would be better served to observe your dog closely and teach them a handful of other behaviours to sharpen your skills while you learn their language.

My biggest objection is that, in the early stages of housetraining, your dog really shouldn't be far enough away from you to need a noisy way to signal you. By the time they're ready for that kind of responsibility, you will likely know them well enough to understand when they need to go out.

Automatic Signals

Sometimes, a dog's way of saying they need to go out looks a lot like everything else they have to say. We are currently raising an Irish Setter, and she is quite possibly the world's happiest dog. When she was very young, we taught her to carry things in her mouth so that small children could pet her safely. If she finds a favourite toy (or, to be honest, a shoe, a bit of lint, or something our cat dragged in) she will pick it up and show it to everyone in the house, all the while making her feet extra thumpy and wagging her tail furiously.

If she heads downstairs with it in her mouth, it either means that she heard a bedroom door open and needs to share the wonder of it all with more people or that she is at the front door and **really needs to pee right now.** We are only just beginning to understand when the thumpy feet and full body-wagging signal desperation rather than love for all humankind.

Yes, we could teach her to ring a bell, but that assumes that she's self-aware enough to know she needs to go in time to call us. When she's engaged with something at the front end ("OMG everyone, look! There's a random thing in my mouth—it's the best thing ever!"), she

Housetraining That Works

has almost no awareness of anything happening at the other end. Very normal for a not-quite-eight-month-old puppy.

In situations where a dog clearly understands where to go but has trouble summoning help, my favourite tools are motion-activated tacky lawn ornaments that make stupid sounds.* A quick search on-line will show you plastic frogs and ducks that croak or quack as your dog walks near them. If you install one by a problematic exit door or set of stairs, you will be alerted if your dog is in the area.

Motion detectors are also very helpful in cases where there's a history of a dog having accidents in remote parts of the house.

Congratulations! You've made it through all seven steps, and your dog is well on their way to being housetrained. If you're training a puppy, they will need time to grow and mature. Other than that, all that remains is to prevent rehearsal of behaviours you don't want and to maintain your potty protocols long enough for their new skills to become habit. It really is that simple.

---

* Oh, sure, you can buy normal-looking sensors that make ordinary sounds, but where's the fun in that? There's a practical side to the whimsy, too. If there's a member of your household with any degree of hearing loss, soft electronic sounds are as easy to miss as slightly thumpier paws.

CHAPTER 12

Handling Accidents

What If My Dog Has an Accident?

Clean it up.

Stay calm.

Most importantly, don't punish your dog. Not even if you catch them in the act.

Housetraining accidents are more of a "when" than an "if." It isn't the end of the world, and you haven't failed. While it's true that most accidents are actually handler errors, they are also very important data. Logging when they happen, where they happen and what you were doing at the time will help you adjust your timings and show you where you need to tighten up on supervision and confinement.

No matter where, when or why the accident occurred, your response should be the same. Clean it, log it and *look for patterns*.

Types of Accident

Most accidents fall into two categories. No, not *those* two! Usually, if you find an unsanctioned puddle or pile, the occurrence is timing-related or owner behaviour-related. Either way, logging your dog's potty activities will usually point you to a solution.

Timing accidents happen most when you haven't yet learned how your dog's individual system works. Or you have a puppy and their timings keep changing as they grow. If you consistently take them out at 10:30 AM and nothing happens, but somewhere between 11:00 and 11:15 you find an accident, then you know to start taking your dog out at 10:45. If they don't go, try again at 11:00. No matter how much they say they don't have to go, absolutely do not let them be loose in the house.

By far the most common reason for accidents is owner inattention. It's a really good idea to log what you were doing at the time of the accident. It might be you were getting the kids out the door for school. Maybe a friend called and you got busy chatting. Or there might possibly have been a digital screen involved. You'd be amazed at how many dogs recognize that, if you're looking at a screen, they will never be able to get your attention, so they might as well just go pee. For dogs who have been punished, any sound your device makes quickly becomes a signal that no one will be watching them and it's safe to sneak off for a potty break.

Once you know the type of accident, it's fairly easy to prevent repeat occurrences by adjusting your timings, rearranging their environment or, best of all, managing your own behaviour.

If you're getting kids off to school, maybe tuck puppy into their crate with their breakfast or even hold off on giving breakfast until all the

Handling Accidents

small humans are out the door. Make a habit of setting a timer when your dog is having free time. Bring them into a smaller area and shut the door if you're on the phone. And, no exceptions, if you're going to be looking at a screen, set a timer *and* confine your dog—even if that just means having them on leash beside you. (Excuse me for a moment—I have to go put an Irish Setter puppy on a leash.)

Cleaning Up

Regardless of how vigilant you are, the occasional accident is inevitable. You're going to need a cleaning kit. If your house is large, consider having one on each floor. If your dog goes to work with you, have one there. Speaking as someone who has been a mom, a grandmother, a caregiver for an elderly parent and a multiple dog owner, keep one in the car too.

What goes in the kit? At a minimum, you'll need poo bags, paper towels, wet wipes and a good enzyme-based cleaner. Your home kit should probably have a dustpan and a scraper of some sort because sooner or later you'll have to scrape up something more liquid than solid. (Don't try to grab it with poo bags, just scrape it into the dustpan and pour it down the toilet.) Mops with easily removable/washable heads are also really useful. Your car kit should probably have a garbage bag and a change of clothes too.

The right cleaning products make all the difference. Please don't bother with anything from the grocery store. A lot of them contain ammonia, which is one of the ingredients in urine and will attract your dog back to the area. Be careful about the ones at the pet supply store too. Most are ineffective at best and a surprising number of them also have ammonia.

Housetraining That Works

There are really only a few cleaners worth bothering with. First up is good old budget-friendly white vinegar mixed 50/50 with water. It does the job just fine for recent messes but is limited in what it can do for anything that's been there a while, and some folks really object to the smell.

Enzyme-based cleaners can be found in any good pet supply store. There are some good ones that will handle most messes and others that are a waste of a spray bottle. Nature's Miracle is pretty much the industry standard and easy to find on my side of the pond. Get the extra strength if it's available. You may prefer the unscented one. The scented isn't awful and most dogs don't seem to mind it, but it loses its appeal after the first fifty pee spots. If possible, just buy the gallon jug. You're going to want to add some to your mop bucket and to your washer when doing pet laundry.

My all-time favourite product has a rather silly name but works like nothing else—probably because it uses both enzymes and live bacteria. Non-toxic and pet-friendly "Anti-Icky-Poo" handles everything from forensic situations to skunk spray, and it's the only thing that really works on cat pee. (We once used it to successfully de-stink a house that was previously occupied by cat-hoarding chain smokers.) It has seen us through freezer malfunctions, epic diarrhea and road trips with carsick dogs. I've even been known to spray it directly on my dogs after they've rolled in bear crap or rotten fish—two things that often go together in my neck of the woods. Probably the best feature is that it keeps working even after it dries. This amazing product is a little harder to find but well worth the effort.

If neither Nature's Miracle or Anti-Icky-Poo is available in your area, your best bet is to look for an on-line supplier that caters to boarding kennels, groomers and breeders.

Handling Accidents

You may have noticed that bleach is not on my list. That's because, although it's a very effective and budget-friendly disinfectant, there are some real downsides. Use extreme caution when cleaning puppy areas with bleach. If there's any residual bleach, it can create chlorine gas when puppies pee on it. That can be lethal if the gas is trapped under bedding or paper and a puppy burrows underneath. If you need to disinfect puppy areas, you would be better off using a commercial kennel disinfectant. If you must use bleach, please make sure that you rinse thoroughly.

Super Important Pro Tip:

Keep your mouth shut when bending over to clean accidents. Yes, I know you're frustrated, and you probably want to vent a little, but stuff splatters. Take it from me and learn this the easy way.

Why We Don't Punish

If you find a puddle or a pile where there shouldn't be one, it's too late to do anything about it. We've come a long way from the days where all the books said you had to drag the poor dog over to the mess, scold them, whack them on the rump with a rolled-up newspaper or rub their nose in the mess. Yuck! (If this is news to you, I promise not to tell anyone if you promise never to do it again.)

Although training in general has advanced quite a bit, there are still a lot of people under the impression that it's okay to punish a dog for accidents as long as you catch them in the act. The usual advice is to scold the dog and then take it outside. Small problem—they're empty now, so it's just you and your dog standing around accomplishing nothing. If you can catch your dog in the act, maybe just aim to catch them three seconds *before* the accident. Then you can take them outside and reward the right behaviour.

The challenge here is that to reward pottying outside, we need to be able to see them doing it. When a dog is punished for going to the bathroom in the house, they almost never make the connection that it's the actual going to the bathroom that's getting them in trouble. They are much more likely to think that *being seen by you* is the issue. Or that it's just that one spot that is off limits. Or maybe it's just that room. Or just the rooms with carpets. Or just downstairs. Until the only place left is at the very back of your closet where your really expensive shoes are. (Care to guess how that owner found out?) That's how you end up with a "sneaky" dog.

"Sneaky," in this case, really means "dog who is desperately trying not to offend you." You can easily tell if you have one—just take your dog outside when you know they really have to go. If you end up standing there while your dog putters around aimlessly or just metaphorically crosses its legs and refuses to go, it's highly likely there's been a history of punishment or scolding.

When you finally give up and bring your dog inside, all it takes is for you to turn your back for an instant, and now there's a puddle or a pile on the floor. And that's going to make you feel like punishing your dog. (Which you won't do because now you are an enlightened owner and know that will make it worse.)

It's very frustrating, and you get buckets of sympathy, but it's up to the humans involved to fix this. No more punishing, no more scolding. If you're really grumpy about having found another mess, quietly put your dog somewhere else while you clean up because the faces that you make can be as upsetting as direct scolding.

Handling Accidents

While we're on the subject, can we deal with that whole "he knows he's done wrong and he's acting guilty" thing? Your dog knows no such thing. What looks like guilt to human eyes is just appeasement behaviour in the face of perceived aggression. Most often it shows up the minute you spot the mess, but some dogs will start grovelling before you even find it. It's very easy to think that your dog knows he's done wrong, but that just isn't the case. What happens is that you "complete the circuit" of the behaviour. If you had a camera watching your dog, you'd only see the "guilty" behaviour when you arrived home or came into the vicinity. For your dog, the two equations are simple:

1. poop or pee inside + no human = relief
2. poop or pee inside + human = bad news for dog

Housetraining is usually the very beginning of your training journey with your dog. Regardless of how far you want to go with their education, starting off assuming the worst about them makes for an adversarial relationship. That is not an ideal foundation for a happy life together.

Going forward, please assume your dog is doing the best they can with the information and skills they have.

Parting Thoughts

Congratulations on completing the first leg of your training journey and thank you so much for allowing me to be a part of your dog's education. Working together with your pup, you have forged the beginnings of a lifelong partnership based on love, trust and understanding.

This is where I'm supposed to give you a quick pat on the back, wish you luck and hint about future books before saying goodbye, but I can't quite bring myself to let you go without showing you just how far you've come and casting a vision for where you might go next.

Let's review what you've learned so far:

- ☐ I learned how to use a house leash or drag line
- ☐ I learned why dogs have accidents
- ☐ I learned how dogs learn
- ☐ I learned why *my* dog was having accidents
- ☐ I learned how to set up potty areas and confinement areas
- ☐ I learned how to teach a potty cue
- ☐ I learned how to do a potty run
- ☐ I learned how to design a potty plan
- ☐ I learned how to teach my dog new behaviours

Bonus points:

- ☐ I'm so good at "being a tree" that small birds try to build nests on me
- ☐ My new hobby is re-writing popular songs to sing to my dog during potty runs

Well done! That's a whole lot of new knowledge and skills. You may not yet realize just how big a deal that is, but when you take your dog to a training class, any instructor worth their salt will notice right away that you and your dog are a team with serious potential.

Sneaky Trainer Behaviour Roundup

I've mentioned a time or two that trainers are a sneaky lot. We love teaching big, important things in bite-sized pieces that are barely noticeable. We'll let the dog think they're training us (which is truer than you might want to know). Or we'll let you think we're just working on some basic housetraining skills.

Confession time: most of the behaviours taught in this book have benefits far beyond housetraining. Some of them build trust. Some of them are really important parts of core behaviours like coming when called or learning to stay. Some of them will lend themselves towards fitness and rehab should your dog ever be injured or have arthritis when they're older. Some of them are designed to give you a foundation for nose work or for competitive dog sports. I chose behaviours that were easy but also behaviours that have a lot of room for growth.

Let's take a look at the behaviours we've covered so far and see which ones are foundations for more advanced skills.

Parting Thoughts

☐ I taught my dog to go to the bathroom on leash
☐ I taught my dog a potty cue

Okay, I admit it—there's not a whole lot more you can do with these two. It's not like there are contests for on-leash pottying prowess, but if there were, you and your dog would be medalists. Also, it's impossible to teach either of these without first establishing a level of trust, and that's a solid foundation for everything else.

☐ I taught my dog a marker signal

This is huge. If your dog understands marker signals, there's no limit to what you can teach them. You might even consider adding a couple more marker signals for different types of behaviours. For instance, I often use clickers for complicated behaviours, and I have a couple different verbal markers—one for calm behaviours, one for scent work and, for everything else, good old "Yes!"

☐ I taught my dog "Four on the Floor"

On the surface, this is just a way to prevent the behaviour of jumping up. That's reason enough to teach it, but it will also teach your dog "indirect access." That is, it's a great way for your dog to learn that the best way to get what they want isn't just to hurl themselves at it repeatedly.

When dogs are first learning this, they usually back up a little bit. They quite often will make eye contact with you or offer another position— these can all get marked with a prompt "Yes!" and then rewarded. Over time, you can add verbal cues or hand signals and "capture" a new behaviour. Sometimes you'll be offered behaviours you don't want— such as barking, whining or pawing at you—and, because you're a behaviour-shaping whiz now, your dog will learn right from the start that those things cause you to get distracted and forget how to open the door or give treats.

This seemingly basic exercise has benefits far beyond the obvious one of not having your dog knock people over or cover you in mud. The really important part is they learn to think about what they're doing and whether it's working or not working. They learn that trying something new is not only safe but desirable and that the worst that can happen is they might not get what they want. Four on the Floor is a powerful foundation behaviour that teaches self-control, creativity and volunteerism.

☐ I taught my dog "Noses"

We started teaching this mostly to make it easier and faster to get a wiggly puppy "dressed" to go out to potty. Then it just becomes a cute bonding moment to have your dog run to you to have their collar put on. You might never take it further, but you might also grow the behaviour to include fetching their leash and collar before going out.

If you decide to introduce your dog to a harness, using the "Noses" cue will make it easier for your dog to understand that a harness is just an elaborate collar that extends to their body.

When they've adapted to harness, it's just one small step more to introduce backpacks. Wouldn't it be nice if they could carry their own gear on longer walks or hikes?

Perhaps the most surprising benefit of this behaviour is how large a part it plays in teaching your dog to come when called. There is a concept in behaviour shaping that says the last part, or the most important part, of a behaviour sequence should get

Parting Thoughts

taught first. Being able to get hold of your dog when they come to you is both the last part and the most important part. Guess what you've been inadvertently practicing every time you put your dog's collar on? Yup—getting your dog comfortable with you holding their collar.

Lots of dogs will joyfully run towards their owner—and then zoom straight past them. Over and over again. By teaching your dog a positive association with you taking hold of their collar, you have positioned yourself to successfully teach your dog to reliably come when called. You can start now to grow that behaviour when your dog comes to put their collar on by saying their name as they move towards you, holding their collar a little longer, letting go of it and taking hold of it again before giving the treat or even trotting backwards a few steps as they approach.

☐ I taught my dog "Puppy Zen"

This is the ultimate indirect access game. This is where they learn that the best way to get what they want isn't to just tackle it or throw themselves at it but to figure out what behaviour they can do for us to get permission or access.

Let's say, for instance, that your dog wants to go play with another dog. You've already taught your pup that in order to get the treat, they must not try to get the treat and, perhaps, that in order to get the toy, they must not try to get the toy. It's an easy next step to teach them that in order to go play with the other dog, they must pay attention to you first. Which can be grown to playing with you first. Which then makes you more fun than other dogs.

Puppy Zen can be grown to so many things. It teaches indirect access, waiting for permission, self control and offering alternate behaviours. It teaches them to keep trying—and that you're not just a big meanie who won't let them have any fun. At some point, the very act of withholding something they want will signal them that this is a training situation with potential for a payoff if they don't allow themselves to be distracted.

☐ I taught my dog that stillness gets rewarded

That tiny little moment of self control we ask before we let them out of the crate or x-pen can be used in any number of situations. We can ask for stillness when they're on a station or when we're grooming or before we release them to go play. If you are really clear with your dog that the release and reward happens when they are still for a nano-second, even the wiggliest of dogs will learn to take a breath and control themselves before rocketing off to the next event.

If you have a high-energy, zoom-through-life, tap-dancing kind of dog, it is a really amazing thing to see them consciously choose to be still for a moment instead of just leaping around madly.

Teaching them these micro-pauses gives them a chance to "read the room," to notice that you are still and adjust their behaviour accordingly.

Brief moments of deliberate stillness are also the precursor to teaching them to Stay.

☐ I taught my dog a release word

This one is a little different because the release word itself doesn't grow into something bigger.

Parting Thoughts

It's more that the behaviours your dog is released from can grow simply because there is a release word.

It's all very well and good to have a dog who will do what you ask, but if they can just decide to wander off anytime they want, the usefulness of those behaviours is questionable. A release word is the secret sauce that allows you to build duration and reliability.

☐ I taught my dog to lure

Basic "follow the cookie" luring is an essential foundation skill, but when your dog is more advanced you won't use it very often. What you'll do instead is grow the basic behaviour into empty hand luring and "taking a directional" (going beyond your hand to somewhere you pointed). You can even grow it to include directed retrieving (please bring me the duck on the left).

Whether you're teaching your dog to navigate an agility obstacle, sending them to a platform to wait their turn, helping them find an easier way into a vehicle or pointing out which sheep you need to shear next, you will use this skill so often that eventually you will just take it for granted that your dog will go where you ask with the slightest of gestures (sometimes just a flick of your eyes or a tilt of your head).

☐ I taught my dog to "Step Up"

This one is a favourite of mine because it's the starting point for so many skills. Depending on the dog and the day, you might teach multiple behaviours with one object (all four feet on, stepping down, leaving their back feet on, backing up to place hind feet) or introduce a second object (front feet on one, hind feet on the other) and work up to a trail of objects or one object for each paw.

Or you might just stick with one object and add some work on distance or duration.

If you're working on distance and duration, it's called "stationing," and if there's fancy footwork involved, it's called "perch work."

Stationing is really about self-control. It is most useful when your dog has to be calm or hold position while something exciting is happening. It might be guests at the door, another dog having a turn or your kid's soccer practice.

Perch work is more about fitness and self-knowledge. Many dogs have a very limited understanding of how to move well or even where their feet are at any given moment. Mastering their own body will give them a whole new skill set to enhance their fitness, prevent injuries and prepare them for advanced work like agility or backpacking. It's also a great confidence builder and brain workout.

☐ I taught my dog "Ready?"

"Ready" can be either the cue for eye contact or just a shorthand to describe the behaviour. It means "if you want that exciting thing over there, please give me your eyeballs." You may have started with just asking for a flicker of eye contact before taking your dog out to potty, but that's just the beginning.

If you consistently ask your dog to make eye contact before they get access to something they want, they will learn to pay very close attention to you when they're around distractions. It's also useful for getting your dog past scary or problematic things so you can give them an alternate reward when they're safely past the danger. You get extra smarty-pants points if you figured out this is another indirect access exercise.

Parting Thoughts

For most of my own dogs, I make eye contact be the default behaviour (no cue needed), but I also teach them a cue for looking straight ahead when I want them to keep an eye on something for me (usually a sheep contemplating a creative escape). This is also a great option for dogs who live in urban settings where they might have to deal with walking past reactive dogs, friendly people and urban wildlife.

If your dog is going to have a hunting or agility career, it's probably more useful to make the default behavior be looking straight ahead with "Ready?" as the cue for them to give you eye contact.

☐ I taught my dog to back up

Yes, this is a behaviour that can be grown into some really impressive tricks (freestyle dance, handstands, positioning for catching a disc), but it's also seriously useful as a stand-alone behaviour.

It's easy to overlook how handy it is to have a dog who will back up on cue until you spend time with a dog who doesn't know how. Whether you're competing and need to adjust your start line or you're posing them for a picture or you just need them to scooch back a bit so you can put their bowl down, it is unbelievably useful to be able to adjust your dog's position by having them back up a few steps rather than having to lead them in a big circle.

☐ I taught my dog to wait

"Wait" is a self control exercise and a safety exercise. For me if there's a door involved, the default is that they should wait until given permission to exit, but it's also really helpful to have a dog who knows what a verbal "Wait" cue means.

Housetraining That Works

For clarity, "Wait" and "Stay" are not the same thing. "Wait" means don't dive for the thing, don't go ahead of me, please hang out in this general area, pause before we cross the street or while I tie my shoelaces. "Stay" means stay in the exact place I put you in, do not change position.

Whether you teach wait on cue, as a default behaviour or both, you will be helping your dog learn self-control. Dogs who know how to wait will have an easier time learning formal stays.

That's a no-brainer, but did you know that dogs who can stay put in the face of distractions are also much more likely to come when they're called? And that dogs who know how to stay and come when called are easier to teach leash manners? That's because you've already shown them that self-control gets rewarded and that you are a reliable source of good things.

Go Team Awesome!

Now that you know just how amazing you are, take some time to think about what you'd like your dog to know six months from now and what your next steps should be. Is there a simple job you could give your dog? Is there a handful of tricks you'd like to teach? Would you benefit from taking a class? Maybe private lessons would be a good choice.

Whatever you choose, please treat their education as a lifelong adventure rather than a "one and done" event. May the two of you have many happy years together. (And, yes, there will be another book.)

Quick Start Housetraining Guide

If you jumped to this section because you need help right away, please know that everything will be okay. House training is simple but not always easy. There may be times when you wonder why you ever got a dog. All I can tell you is that this phase doesn't last long, it gets easier and, if you do it right the first time, you'll save yourself a lot of time, money and frustration.

Successful housetraining rests on just a few key practices. If you feed your dog a food that agrees with them, give them adequate opportunities to go in the right place, reinforce consistently, supervise effectively and confine them safely when your eyes have to be elsewhere, you will succeed.

Let's get started. First, make sure you can tick all the boxes below. If not, those things will need to be addressed first.

Housetraining That Works

- ☐ My dog appears to be healthy and does not have diarrhea
- ☐ I have a way to confine my dog when I can't supervise them directly
- ☐ I have set up a designated potty area
- ☐ My dog is comfortable wearing a leash and collar (or harness)
- ☐ My dog is at least seven weeks old

If you can't tick off these boxes yet, you might need a trip to the vet, a more gut-friendly food, a quick peek at the chapters on confinement and supervision, or perhaps a small, fenced area for your dog to potty in until the leash and collar become less scary and paralysis inducing. (It's hard to pee when you're frozen with fear or overwhelmed.)

Here's a quick overview before we get started:

In order to housetrain your dog, you need to understand what makes dogs go to the bathroom. Then you need to pick a spot you want them to go and a place to put them between excursions. They need to learn how to go when you take them there, and you have to take them there on a leash and watch to make sure they actually go. If they don't go when you take them to their spot, you will have to either carry or confine them until you try again. Once they're going reliably and you're better at predicting when they need to go out, you get to teach them a cue word for pottying so it's easier to get them empty when you're in a hurry or the weather is nasty. You will praise them and reinforce them for pottying in the right place. At no point will you scold or punish your dog for accidents (aka "handler errors").

Let's get started!

Ever heard of the gastrocolic reflex? That's what makes your dog need to go to the bathroom whenever they eat, drink or chew extensively.

Quick Start Housetraining Guide

You have to be aware of when it gets triggered. In addition, your dog will need to go out when they wake up, after playing, after stress (going to the vet, people arriving or leaving, meeting a dog, getting scared) and just before going to sleep.

☐ I understand what makes my dog need the bathroom.

Whenever one of these triggers occurs, you will need to take your dog out, on leash, to go to the bathroom. Why on a leash? Why can't you just shiver in your bathrobe by the back door, clutching your coffee? Because if you just let them wander around outside having a grand old time until they finally go and then bring them back in, they will quickly learn to hold it longer and longer so they can keep having fun and destroying your yard. Meanwhile, when you realize that you're late for work and bring them inside, they'll potty in the house as soon as you're not looking.

☐ I understand why my dog needs to be taken out on a leash.

The Potty Run

When you get out to the potty area, it's really important that you be really boring. Don't stare at your dog—it's very hard to relax and go to the bathroom with someone staring at you. Look at your dog out of the corner of your eye and keep an eye out for circling or sniffing behavior.

Stand in one spot for three to five minutes and do your best impression of a tree. With a bit of luck, your pup will get bored and relax enough to go.

Praise warmly for every successful outing, but don't get too excited or loud. Yes, you can use treats, but, after the behaviour is established, relief is its own reward. Typically, I give treats for peeing for the first three to five days. Pooping gets rewarded for a little longer because it happens less often. Keep the treats very small as they can backfire by triggering the gastrocolic reflex.

Only time will tell whether or not they also need to have a poo at the same time or, if they pooped, whether they also need to pee. The rule is "No potty, no party." You have to be boring until they go to the bathroom.

When they get the job done and you're sure they're empty, you can play, be silly and tell them they're lovely, fabulous, wonderful! Best dog ever. It's a really good idea at this point to take them for a short walk around the block (if they like walks and it's safe to do so), or to play with them for a while.

If your potty run was successful, you can now go back inside and enjoy a five-to-twenty-minute reprieve. You can allow them a few minutes running free in one room, dragging their house leash, or you can spend a few minutes training before returning to your confinement strategies.

- ☐ I understand how to reinforce my dog for pottying in the right place.
- ☐ I understand how to do a potty run and I am a virtuoso of boring tree-ness.

If they don't go, or just pee when you think they had to poop, it isn't necessary to stand there forever. Three to five minutes will do. Less if it's raining sideways. Bring them back in but supervise closely or confine them until you're ready to try again in half an hour.

Quick Start Housetraining Guide

☐ I understand that I must confine or carry my dog between unsuccessful potty runs.
☐ I understand that it is not possible to supervise effectively while looking at a screen.

Once you've had a few days of no accidents, it's time to introduce a cue for pottying. Please go read Chapter 7. You have time now that you're not constantly cleaning up messes.

Be aware of your dog's food intake. Until they're housetrained, take away any unconsumed food after ten minutes. Feed a good quality diet, whether for you that means kibble, homemade or raw. Watch what goes in his mouth and what comes out the other end. Keep notes and adjust his diet based on results, not opinions.

☐ I understand that what and when my dog eats directly affects housetraining.

Do not scold or swat your dog for having an accident. Under no circumstances rub their noses in it. (I can't believe I actually have to say that.) It will not teach them to be clean, only to hide from you and go when you're not looking (they may even hide the evidence by eating it).

You'll find a handy record-keeping log at the back of this book. Keeping track of what your dog does (and when and where) can be very helpful for seeing patterns. Photocopy or print a couple extra so you have enough to get you through the first two to four weeks.

☐ I understand that there are no accidents, only "handler errors."

If you find an accident, put your dog in their confinement area and clean it up with a good enzyme-based cleaner. Do not use bleach or ammonia-based products. A gallon of enzyme cleaner is a good investment.

It's also really important to keep their potty area clean. Do not ask them to tiptoe through a minefield of poop. Also, It's not unusual for dogs to want to poop in one place and pee in another, especially if they've had a punishment history. If your dog poops and then really wants to get the heck out of Dodge, allow them to move a few feet away to pee.

Always clean up when your dog poops in public. If you get caught without a bag, solemnly promise that you will clean an extra "penalty poop" next time because the Housetraining Fairy knows a lot of tax auditors.

☐ It's a dirty job, but I'll do it.

That's enough information to get you started. When you're ready for more details, please read the rest of the book while your puppy is napping. You can do this.

Resources

Feeding

Whole Dog Journal is an all-around brilliant publication. They accept no advertising and are entirely subscription driven, so they can be trusted to tell it like it is. Subscriptions are affordable and also grant you access to their digital archive. Over the years, their advice has saved me a lot of time, money and heartache. (And, no, they didn't pay me to say this.)

This lovely magazine will give you insights into positive training, equipment and book reviews, helpful information on complementary therapies and, best of all, solid advice on nutrition. If you are feeling overwhelmed by all the contrary opinions about feeding, WDJ will help you advocate for your dog and make the best possible decision for your situation.

whole-dog-journal.com
1-800-424-7887

Housetraining That Works

Body Condition Score

Any number of versions of this are easily found with a quick online search, but this one is particularly helpful because it has separate charts for different sizes of dog.

Go to petmd.com and search for "How to Find Your Dog's Body Condition Score" by Jennifer Coates, DVM.

Cleaning Supplies

My all-time favourite cleaning product for all things biological is MisterMax Anti-Icky-Poo. There is nothing better. If you're housetraining a dog in a home that has a long history of accidents or pet occupation, use this one to give your dog the best chance of success.

mistermax.com
1-800-745-1671

A close second is Shop Care's Super Enzyme Urine and Odor Destroyer. This one is a little more budget-friendly and ideal for cleaning up when the mess is recent. It can be ordered directly from the company. I also highly recommend their laundry detergent.

shopcareproducts.com
1-833-957-0791

In Canada, my favourite place to order this is Dogs Do Smile (aka Continental Pet Company) based in Comox, BC on beautiful Vancouver Island. (Yes, I'm a teensy bit biased.) If you are susceptible to blowing your budget on adorable/gorgeous collars and leashes,

Resources

it's probably safest to just call them, rather than scroll through the website. I have never left their store without either a new collar for the pups or a new and fabulous t-shirt, hoodie or jacket for me. They also have top quality grooming and show dog supplies. You have been warned. If you have trouble finding the cleaner, just enter "enzyme" into the search function.

continentalpetcompany.com
250-702-7578
Dogs Do Smile
266 Anderton Road
Comox, BC V9M 1Y2

Equipment and Toys

Martingale collars and decent leashes can be found fairly easily, but most of the toys sold in pet supply stores are short-lived and designed for dogs to self-entertain. There are always a few fetch and tug toys, but they are rarely made with durability or training in mind. It is my fondest wish that you will continue to build on your housetraining foundation and to educate your dog for years to come.

4 My Merles is my favourite source for toys, leashes and collars. They make good stuff.

4mymerles.com

Supplements

Pain and stiffness affect housetraining both directly and indirectly. Whether from a simple physical inability to access the potty area or from pain-induced anxiety triggering an increase in marking behaviours, the first step in re-training is often pain reduction.

While there are gazillions of pet supplements available with varying degrees of budget-destroying expense and questionable efficacy, one product that stands out for results, quality and reasonable price is Purica Pet Recovery. It's a go-to in our household for cats, dogs and equines. (They make supplements for people, too.)

purica.com
1-877-746-9397 (Canada and USA Toll Free)
(011) 250-746-9397

Resources

Track it to trace it!

Time	Pee or Poop?	Right Spot?	Accident?	If accident, where did it happen and where was I?
:00 :15 :30 :45				
:00 :15 :30 :45				
:00 :15 :30 :45				
:00 :15 :30 :45				
:00 :15 :30 :45				
:00 :15 :30 :45				
:00 :15 :30 :45				
:00 :15 :30 :45				

Acknowledgments

Over the years, I've written a fair amount—homework sheets, essays, articles, short stories and even a handful of poems—but a book is a different creature altogether. I've heard fiction writers complain that their characters often take on a life of their own and refuse to comply with a pre-determined plot.

Foolishly, it never occurred to me that concepts would be similarly inclined. They insisted on talking to each other, repeating themselves and popping up in unexpected or inconvenient places. Then the anecdotes wanted equal attention, but I fobbed off most of them on the promise of a workshop or on-line course later.

In much the same way that non-parents have opinions about child-rearing, folks who don't share their lives with authors have rose-coloured notions about what it's like to be around that level of deranged productivity—which is why readers are often bemused by the lengthy and heartfelt expressions of gratitude at the front or back of a book.

Housetraining That Works

As this project nears completion, I have noticed myself carefully reading other authors' acknowledgements, and I'm now painfully aware of just how many people were affected by this project, how many others were called on for help and how much difference the right workspace can make.

Now it's my turn to thank a long list of people.

Thank you to everyone who pre-ordered a book and then had to wait months longer than expected while I dealt with some life events. You were all so very patient, and it is very much appreciated.

Huge thanks to my home team for putting up with me, covering barn chores, looking after dogs, making me hot drinks, pestering me to hydrate and throwing snacks at me from a safe distance.

Oh, and for sitting across from me at coffee shops while I typed and swore and muttered to myself. (You're probably the reason the authorities weren't called.) It's time for our merry band of travellers to celebrate. Dinner's on me.

To my favourite sailor, thank you for your unwavering confidence in me. Now these chapters are done, let's start a new one of our own. Romance, adventure and happily-ever-after aren't fiction with you by my side.

Taliesin and Ruadh, I promise there will be more walks, more play, more snuggles, more beach and more training now. Yes, Tally, more sheep. Yes, Ruadh, more birds too.

To my Trusted Advisors group—Ann, Rachel, Susan, Wendy, Renee and Kimberlee—thanks for nagging, reading, encouraging and having opinions. Your contributions have been invaluable, and your friendship means the world to me.

Acknowledgments

Thank you to the wonderful staff at Spinnakers in Victoria, BC for making it possible to just hole up and write the whole first draft. I'll be back soon.

Without the Spiral Cafe, also in Victoria, I would probably still be gnashing my teeth over the last three chapters. Two nights of sitting at the back (again with the muttering) during open mic night joggled something loose and solved the whole mess. It really was the "Needed Time."

Huge thanks to every coffee house owner with the forethought and kindness to create a space conducive to writing. I love good coffee, and I love long wooden workbenches. Put the two together and I'm in my happy place.

A large chunk of this book came into being at Saltspring Island Coffee in Ganges, BC, and I can't say enough good things about this welcoming, inclusive place.

Saving my favourite workspace for last, thank you, Joseph and Samantha, for bringing your Coffee Shack to Chemainus, BC. For all the hours I spend there, you should probably just charge me rent. (Natalie, thanks for all those amazing Maple Africanos and for putting up with me wanting my avocado toast just "a little extra toasty for structural reasons.")

This is the part where I worry that I've left someone out (which I almost certainly have) and start frantically listing the bakeries that provided me with writer fuel, the restaurant that got my black bean chicken chow mein just right when I was so tired after that tricky chapter and that nice lady on the bus who told me I should write a book.

Housetraining That Works

It's no use. There will be omissions. I'm sorry. I'll make sure you get included in the next book.

Oh, wait—the dogs! There's no possible way to thank all the dogs who helped me become a better trainer, so I'm appointing a mascot to represent you all. Cedric, I want you and your person to know that I never forgot you. You were seventeen, half-blind, mostly deaf, your feet hurt, your back hurt and you had a heart condition. After spending most of your life being shouted at and locked in a basement, you hated almost everyone. I'll never know what it took for your person to defy her family and get help for you, and I'll never know why you decided to trust me, but I'm so glad you did. You're my greatest housetraining success story. With your snaggle teeth and sticky-out hair, you redefined ugly. But you also redefined brave. It's been at least twenty-five years since we last met, and you've doubtless gone on to your reward. I just wanted you to know that I never forgot you and that I'll love you forever.

About the Author

Zoë MacBean is an eclectic trainer of some 40+ years experience and has never met a stubborn dog—just a whole bunch that were reliable about the wrong things. She's a bit eccentric, perennially scruffy and was pretty much raised in a college psychology lab (which probably explains a lot). When she isn't training dogs, she's either cooking, gardening or having hay picked out of her hair by her very patient husband.

Her dog experience includes a wide range of dog sports—obedience, flyball, agility, musical freestyle, herding and tricks—partly because it's really fun but also because with enough ribbons and certificates on the wall, you don't have to repaint as often. She's also done some guest speaking, clinics and workshops, shelter work, a youth correctional facility dog program and a little movie work.

Zoë decided at age seven to be a trainer and can still remember exactly where she was standing in the school library when she realized that was an option. She studied, volunteered, washed dogs, scooped poop and became a trainer about ten years later (and pretty much kept doing all those things). Other than a year off to work with horses and a brief stint in the reserves, training is how she's earned her keep since then.

She lives on a small farm on Vancouver Island with a weird little blue dog, a foolish young setter, three lazy semi-retired pack goats, too many sheep and a very handsome mule.

Zoë MacBean
Dog Trainer • Author • Housetraining Fairy

"Have leash, will travel."

Housetraining That Works
For Dogs of All Ages, Breeds and Backgrounds

Zoë MacBean

Zoë MacBean likes to talk to people. A lot. Random strangers, small audiences, crowds and anything in between. Mostly about dogs and how changing their behaviour changes us. She's been getting randomly reinforced for talking about dogs for forty years or so. Sometimes she gets invited back and, so far, no one has thrown rotten fruit.

Her dog training experience spans four decades and includes a wide range of dog sports—obedience, flyball, agility, musical freestyle, herding and tricks. She's also done some clinics and workshops, shelter and rescue work, a youth correctional facility dog program and even worked on a couple of movies. Recently, she has taken up field work and rally obedience.

Originally, she specialized in bull breeds and terriers but quickly learned that she enjoys working with opinionated dogs in general. If they've been booted out of dog class or labelled "untrainable," she likes them even more.

Much as she loves dog sports, what gives her the greatest joy is training for its own sake. For the magic that happens when we set aside all the labels and find better ways to respond to the dog in front of us. For the transformation that happens at both ends of the leash when people find the dog they've always wanted inside the dog they have.

Speaker topics:

🐾 Stubborn doesn't exist. How adversarial labels limit our relationships.

🐾 My last dog wasn't like this!—"sur-thriving" your high-needs or neuro-spicy dog.

🐾 Healwork: the training journey as a healing path.

🐾 Who is your dog inviting you to become?

🐾 Right dog, wrong time. Navigating chaos and adversity with a new dog.

Contact Zoë if you would like her to speak at your event

✉ dogstuffthatworks@gmail.com   🌐 housetrainingfairy.com

Want More?

If you'd like to see video tutorials on how to teach all the Sneaky Trainer Bonus Behaviours, please email me and I'll send you a link plus an invitation to a private Facebook group.

Want a little extra help? Looking for next steps in your training journey? Schedule an online coaching session with me and we'll figure it out together.

Have some extra challenges and really want someone to hold your hand through the whole process? Need the Housetraining Fairy to just tell you exactly what to do at each step? Poof! Problem solved. We'll do a live video walk through of your house, get to know your dogs and their unique needs and then design the perfect potty program. Includes follow up coaching sessions to make sure you're successful.

HousetrainingThatWorks@gmail.com

Wingnuttraining.com

Notes

Housetraining That Works

Notes

Housetraining That Works

Notes